THE SEARCH FOR SECURITY
IN POST-TALIBAN AFGHANISTAN

CYRUS HODES AND MARK SEDRA

ADELPHI PAPER 391

The International Institute for Strategic Studies

Arundel House I 13–15 Arundel Street I Temple Place I London I WC2R 3DX I UK

ADELPHI PAPER 391

First published October 2007 by **Routledge**
4 Park Square, Milton Park, Abingdon, Oxon, OX14 4RN

for **The International Institute for Strategic Studies**
Arundel House, 13–15 Arundel Street, Temple Place, London, WC2R 3DX, UK
www.iiss.org

Simultaneously published in the USA and Canada by **Routledge**
270 Madison Ave., New York, NY 10016

Routledge is an imprint of Taylor & Francis, an Informa Business

DIRECTOR-GENERAL AND CHIEF EXECUTIVE John Chipman
EDITOR Patrick Cronin
MANAGER FOR EDITORIAL SERVICES Ayse Abdullah
COPY EDITOR Matthew Foley
ASSISTANT EDITOR Katharine Fletcher
PRODUCTION John Buck
COVER IMAGES Getty Images

Printed and bound in Great Britain by Bell & Bain Ltd, Thornliebank, Glasgow

British Library Cataloguing in Publication Data
A catalogue record for this book is available from the British Library

Library of Congress Cataloging in Publication Data

ISBN 978-0-415-43883-4
ISSN 0567-932X

Contents

Glossary   5

Introduction   7

Part 1: Threats to Security and Stability in Afghanistan

Chapter One   **Warlordism**   11

Chapter Two   **Spoiler Groups and the Anti-government Insurgency**   17
The political, geostrategic, religious and tribal affiliations of
    the Taliban movement   17
The Muttahida Majlis-e-Amal in Pakistan   18
The Taliban as a geostrategic apparatus for Pakistan   19
The border question   20
The FATA and the peace treaties   21
'Hot pursuit'   23
The Kashmir nexus   24
The Taliban's command and control structure   25
Jihadist metastasis: conciliating tribalism and internationalist
    jihad   26
Taliban tactics   27
Jihadist propaganda   28
Taliban PSYOPS   30
Gulbuddin Hekmatyar's Hizb-i Islami (Party of Islam)   30
Al-Qaeda: still there   31
Friendly fundamentalists?   32
Iran's role   33

Chapter Three   **The Opium Trade**   35
An overview of the opium trade   35
The structure of the trade   37
Trafficking routes   38
Corruption   39
The involvement of spoiler groups in the drug trade   39
The counter-narcotics campaign   39
Afghan counter-narcotics institutions   40
The eradication dilemma   41

Part 2: Combating the Threats to Afghanistan's Security

Chapter Four   **International Military Support**   43
Operation Enduring Freedom   43
ISAF and NATO   45
'Ink Spots'   46
Provincial Reconstruction Teams (PRTs)   47
A test for military transformation   49

Chapter Five   **Security-Sector Reform**   51
Military reform   53
Police reform   61
Judicial reform   73
Demilitarisation   83

Conclusion   95

Notes   101

GLOSSARY

ADZ	Afghan Development Zone
AIHRC	Afghan Independent Human Rights Commission
AMF	Afghan Military Force
ANA	Afghan National Army
ANAP	Afghan National Auxiliary Police
ANBP	Afghan New Beginnings Programme
ANP	Afghan National Police
ANSF	Afghan National Security Forces
ATA	Afghan Transitional Authority
CFC-A	Combined Forces Command–Afghanistan
CJTF-76	Combined Joint Task Force-76
CPD	Central Prison Directorate
CPEF	Central Poppy Eradication Force
CNPA	Counter-Narcotics Police of Afghanistan
CSTC-A	Combined Security Transition Command–Afghanistan
CTC	Central Training Center
D&R	Demobilisation and Reintegration Commission
DDR	disarmament, demobilisation and reintegration
DEA	Drug Enforcement Agency (US)
DIAG	Disbandment of Illegal Armed Groups
ETT	Embedded Training Team
ECC	Electoral Complaints Commission
EUPOL	European Policing Mission
GPPO	German Police Project Office
HIG	Hizb-i Islami Gulbuddin
IED	improvised explosive device
IPCB	International Police Coordination Board

ISAF	International Security Assistance Force
ISI	Inter-Services Intelligence Directorate (Pakistan)
KMTC	Kabul Military Training Center
LOTFA	Law and Order Trust Fund for Afghanistan
MMA	Muttahida Majlis-e-Amal (United Action Front)
NDS	National Directorate of Security (Amaniyat)
NIU	National Interdiction Unit
NMAA	National Military Academy of Afghanistan
NWFP	North-West Frontier Province (Pakistan)
OMC-A	Office of Military Cooperation–Afghanistan
OMLT	Operational Mentoring and Liaison Teams
ONSC	Office of the National Security Council
OSC-A	Office of Security Cooperation–Afghanistan
PRD	Police Reform Directorate
PRT	Provincial Reconstruction Team
RTC	Regional Training Center
SSR	security-sector reform
UAV	unmanned aerial vehicle
UNAMA	United Nations Assistance Mission in Afghanistan
UNDP	United Nations Development Programme
UNODC	United Nations Office on Drugs and Crime
UNOPS	United Nations Office for Project Services
USAID	US Agency for International Development
UXO	unexploded ordnance
VBIED	vehicle-borne improvised explosive device

INTRODUCTION

The year 2002 was one of great optimism and hope in Afghanistan. Taliban forces had been routed by the US-led Coalition and its Northern Alliance allies, prompting many to proclaim the demise of the movement. A conference in Bonn had chosen an interim government and produced a blueprint for the country's political transition. A subsequent donor meeting in Tokyo resulted in pledges of approximately $5.2 billion to underwrite reconstruction. Promises by US President George W. Bush and then UK Prime Minister Tony Blair to deliver a 'Marshall Plan' for Afghanistan, and not to abandon the country as the West had done after the Soviet withdrawal in 1989, bred tremendous optimism among ordinary Afghans.

More than five years on, in 2007, this optimism has been replaced by a sense of pessimism. Despite some significant achievements in the reconstruction process, for many Afghans the most noticeable change since the fall of the Taliban regime has been deteriorating security. Many parts of the country, particularly in the south and east, cannot be classified as being in a post-conflict situation. Taliban-led insurgent activity has intensified every year since 2001. By September 2006, an average of 600 insurgent and/or terrorist incidents were occurring every month, up from an average of 130 a month in 2005.[1] There were 139 suicide bombings in 2006, compared to 27 the previous year.[2] In all, the insurgency resulted in over 3,700 fatalities in 2006, more than four times the figure for 2005.[3] Casualty rates continued to rise in 2007, with the Afghan Interior Ministry reporting that 1,060 civilians had been killed between April and August alone.[4] Poor governance, marked by rampant corruption, has been one of the main drivers of insecurity, as increasing numbers of disillusioned Afghans turn to regional commanders and the Taliban to provide basic public goods. The burgeoning drug trade has further fuelled violence, and threatens to transform Afghanistan into a narco-mafia state.

Afghanistan's security crisis can be traced back to the early approach taken by donors, particularly the United States. When the US intervened in Afghanistan in 2001, it did so to overthrow the Taliban and prevent the country from once again serving as a sanctuary for terrorist groups like al-Qaeda. The aim was not to transform the state or consolidate a certain type of peace. As a result, the state-building process, at least in its early stages, was critically under-resourced; as one scholar puts it, the United States and its allies were trying to 'carry out major strategic change on the cheap'.[5] This under-investment applied both to aid for reconstruction and to stabilisation and counter-insurgency operations. The failure to expand the UN-mandated International Security Assistance Force (ISAF) outside the capital in 2002 permitted warlords to consolidate their authority, the Taliban to regroup and drug-traffickers to re-establish their networks. The lack of international troops also placed unreasonable pressure on the nascent security-sector reform (SSR) process. Instead of seeking to create an accountable, equitable and rights-respecting security system, the process became a grandiose train-and-equip programme, whose main objective was to get Afghan security forces 'into the fight', thereby easing the burden on international troops.

By 2004, as the insurgency gained momentum and the drug trade grew to unprecedented proportions, the Afghan government and donors had begun to grasp the implications of this under-investment in the reconstruction process. In response, an international donor conference was convened in Berlin to secure fresh commitments of troops and development aid, and new structures such as Provincial Reconstruction Teams (PRTs) were developed. However, such measures were inadequate to address prevailing problems. The deployment of the PRTs, comprising small groups of military and civil-affairs personnel, reflected the lack of political will among NATO states to commit the necessary resources for a full expansion of ISAF, more than a genuine desire to improve security outside Kabul. PRTs tended only to meet their objectives and achieve a degree of success in already stable areas of the country, primarily in the north. Meanwhile, although the Berlin conference recognised the pivotal nature of the SSR process, it did not result in the funding boost necessary to overcome the major obstacles to reform.

Perhaps the most important development in 2004 was the expansion in the US role in the SSR process. This reflected a wider, albeit tardy, change to embrace state-building more broadly. By 2007, the United States had become the largest donor to four of the five pillars of the SSR process. While this has addressed some of the funding shortfalls, the US fixation with short-term security goals has exacerbated existing problems in the sector, including fiscal sustainability and governance.

This paper charts the evolution of the security environment in Afghanistan. It is divided into two sections. The first explores the prevailing threats to security and stability, including warlordism, spoiler groups, the Taliban-led insurgency, the opium trade and the criminal economy. Section 2 analyses the efforts that have been made to combat these threats, notably international military engagement and the SSR process. A number of themes cut across the two sections of the paper. First and foremost is the issue of external engagement, most notably in relation to Pakistan. The Taliban found sanctuary in Pakistan following its ousting, and used the largely autonomous border regions to regroup and reorganise. While the Pakistani military and the Inter-Services Intelligence Directorate (ISI) have captured or killed numerous high-ranking al-Qaeda figures, Pakistan has largely turned a blind eye to the Taliban, and may even be providing them with clandestine support. Pakistan's apparent double game with regard to the Taliban has been a major driver of insecurity and instability in Afghanistan.

The second cross-cutting theme relates to the lack of coordination and the absence of common aims amongst the main security stakeholders. This has prevented the formation of a coherent and effective strategy to confront insecurity. There are as many interests as stakeholders in the Afghan security sphere, and they often clash. Some donors have inadvertently sacrificed the long-term goal of the state-building process, namely the creation of a stable and self-sufficient Afghan state (an outcome that meets donors' strategic goals) to meet more short-term interests. For instance, the US-led Coalition's use of Afghan militia proxies, some of which are in open opposition to the state, has emboldened potential spoilers and undercut the internationally sponsored demilitarisation process.

The final over-arching theme can be described as the 'political-will problem'. State-building in such a complex setting, with a multiplicity of interests at stake, demands difficult choices by all stakeholders. The government and the international community have not demonstrated the political will to take some of these decisions, whether it is the government's reluctance to purge warlords and drug-traffickers from government positions or the international community's reticence about deploying the necessary troops and resources to stabilise the country.

Afghans are losing faith in a political order which they believe has delivered little, and which has not marked a decisive break with the past. Many do not see the international commitment as durable, and point to the huge disparity in resources allocated to Iraq as opposed to Afghanistan. As the prominent Pakistani journalist Ahmed Rashid has put it: 'In Kabul today, most Afghans, from illiterate cooks to well-educated civil servants, take it for granted that the Taliban are coming back to power'.[6] Stopping this from happening will call for increased levels of assistance from donors and greater political will on the part of the Afghan government to undertake the contentious and painful reforms necessary to bring about genuine change. As this paper shows, the security sphere will remain a locus of attention for Afghanistan's state-builders; without security, the country's ongoing development and political transition cannot move forward.

Part 1: Threats to Security and Stability in Afghanistan

CHAPTER ONE

Warlordism

Warlordism presents one of the most pronounced and confounding challenges to the Afghan state-building process. The mere act of defining a warlord is contentious and complicated. Identifying warlords is a highly subjective process: one person's warlord is another's legitimate political leader. Nonetheless, some common characteristics can be identified. Antonio Giustozzi defines warlords as 'military leaders who emerge to play a *de facto* political role, despite their lack of full legitimacy'.[1] Warlords often collect taxes and customs duties; they maintain their own private armies and exploit the criminal economy. Their power is rooted in the military assets at their disposal, the clientelistic networks they run and, to a lesser extent, outside support.

Afghanistan's contemporary class of warlords are a product of the civil war (1979–2001) and the breakdown of central authority it caused. This period saw a major shift in village political and social hierarchies. Young military commanders usurped traditional governance structures and sources of authority, whether tribal or religious leadership or customary bodies like the village *shura* or *jirga*.[2] In the absence of a functioning state, these actors controlled the distribution of resources at the local level, and provided rudimentary public services. While ethnic, tribal or sectarian solidarity conferred a degree of legitimacy on some of these actors, the dominant characteristic of Afghanistan's warlords is their predatory behaviour towards local communities. The high degree of acceptance and even popularity that the Taliban enjoyed during their rise to power in the mid 1990s stemmed from their success in marginalising these figures – a lesson that the post-Taliban political order did not adequately heed.

Rather than sidelining the warlords and restoring the power and authority of the state, the Bonn Agreement of 2001 sought to accommodate them instead.[3] Barnett Rubin has characterised the political transition launched at Bonn as a form of 'warlord democratisation', in which the dominant strategy has been to co-opt rather than exclude armed commanders.[4] The Bonn Agreement missed an unprecedented opportunity to emasculate Afghanistan's warlords. In late 2001 and early 2002, these figures had yet to re-establish their fiefdoms or consolidate their positions. The proxy relationships that they maintained with external states were largely frozen as patrons assessed how the US would act. Yet far from marginalising or even containing these commanders, the international community enabled them to extend their authority into the heart of the state, giving them a virtual veto over elements of the state-building process.

The government's policy of bringing warlords into the government has weakened the state's capacity for reform and service delivery as modernisers and reformers have been shunted aside in favour of unqualified commanders and their cliques. It has also undermined the legitimacy of the post-war political dispensation. As Giustozzi states, President Hamid Karzai 'could lose in legitimacy what he gains in political power' from his alliances with the old warlord elite.[5] Much of the population identifies these figures with the destruction of the state, rather than with its renewal. Their presence in the government might buy short-term stability in some areas, but it has exacerbated a deeply rooted suspicion of the state that could hinder the extension of its sovereignty over the long term. Moreover, warlords have utilised their positions to colonise parts of the public administration and security forces, particularly sub-national governance bodies and the police.[6] Equally, Karzai could also lose in political power what he gains in legitimacy from his close relations with international partners, as they are also unpopular with portions of the population. Such are the difficult choices he faces.

The international community has been complicit in Karzai's accommodationist approach to the warlords. The United States in particular has favoured the formation of alliances with regional commanders to maintain security and stability until the Afghan National Security Forces (ANSF) are trained and equipped. It has also established proxy relationships with commanders in eastern and southern Afghanistan to support Coalition military operations.

One of the most obvious effects of the reconstitution of warlord power has been the emergence of competition over territory and resources, competition which has often degenerated into violence. The most notable clashes occurred in 2002 and 2003 in northern Afghanistan between the forces of two prominent allies of the government: Rashid Dostum, the leader of the Uzbek-dominated group Junbish-e Milli-ye Islami, and Atta Mohammad, a prominent figure in the largely Tajik Jamaat-e-Islami. Although the conflict has been contained thanks to the intervention of the central government and the international community, tensions persist, and while the insurgency has clearly come to overshadow the threat posed to security by warlord violence, periodic clashes among government-allied commanders remain a problem. For instance, in October 2006, fighting between rival commanders of two Pashtun clans in the western province of Herat killed 32 people and left numerous others injured.[7]

In 2004, prominent international donors such as Japan, Britain and the European Commission began to exert greater pressure on the government to deal with recalcitrant commanders. Defence Minister Marshal Mohammad Qasim Fahim, one of the most powerful commanders in the country and the head of one of the most corrupt ministries in the government, was an obvious target. Fahim was removed from office in the run-up to the presidential elections in October 2004. After the announcement of the decision, ISAF forces in Kabul were placed on alert in anticipation of a coup attempt. It never materialised, convincing many that the scope for government action to confront the warlords was far greater than had been assumed. Another powerful figure, Ismail Khan, the self-proclaimed Emir of Herat, was removed in September 2004 following a wave of fighting around Herat. Khan subsequently accepted the post of minister of energy and water in the government in Kabul, drawing him away from his provincial power base. While proponents of a tougher stance towards armed commanders were emboldened by these developments, Karzai was reluctant to abandon his accommodationist approach, which suited his leadership style. In 2006, following a series of riots in Kabul, Karzai reappointed Fahim to a government position as his security adviser. There has been speculation that the riots were partly orchestrated by supporters of Fahim's Tajik-dominated political faction, Shura-i Nezar, who were angered by the declining influence of Tajiks in the government. Karzai is alleged to have told Western diplomats that removing Fahim was the worst mistake he had made as president, and he blamed the international community for the misjudgement.[8]

A striking example of the deleterious effects of this accommodationist strategy on the state-building process concerns the parliamentary elections in September 2005. Afghanistan's electoral law (Art. 15, No. 3) 'prohibits anyone who commands or belongs to an unofficial military force or armed group from becoming a candidate'. A rigorous vetting process was established to review candidates, and a list of 1,024 individuals with potential links to armed groups was compiled by the Demobilisation and Reintegration Commission, which maintains a countrywide data-base of illegal armed groups. This list was passed to the independent Electoral Complaints Commission (ECC). However, only 34 candidates were excluded from the ballot due to links to armed groups.[9] The Afghan Independent Human Rights Commission (AIHRC), an independent body established by the Bonn Agreement and later mandated by the constitution to monitor the observation of human rights and promote their protection, claimed that over 80% of the winning candidates in the provinces and 60% of successful candidates in Kabul had links to armed groups.[10]

Turnout in the parliamentary elections was sharply down on the presi-dential polls, from 8.1 million to 6.4m. Some observers attribute this fall to public disillusionment over the inclusion in the electoral process of warlords and other figures with questionable pasts.[11] A public-opinion survey[12] conducted in the run-up to the legislative elections by the Kabul-based Human Rights Research and Advocacy Consortium (HRRAC), a group of 15 Afghan and international non-governmental organisations working in the country, found that Afghans were deeply concerned that local commanders, warlords and war criminals would enter parlia-ment.[13] Nonetheless, Karzai favoured allowing a wide range of candidates to stand, including individuals accused of human-rights abuses, on the basis that this would advance national reconciliation. This approach, which was tacitly endorsed by the international community, also stemmed from concerns that, if armed actors were barred from the elections, they would oppose the central government, breaking up the fragile network of disparate groups that Karzai had meticulously constructed. As one UN diplomat stated, the international community was reluctant to authorise disqualifications that would 'undermine the entire process'.[14]

The failure to adequately vet candidates has damaged the parlia-ment at a crucial stage in its development. Allowing warlords to stand in the elections provided another avenue for them to extend their reach into the state and protect their interests. Parliament's standing commit-tees, which provide oversight of the executive, have been dominated by former jihadi commanders, while better-qualified individuals have been excluded. Meanwhile, on 1 February 2007, a motion was passed grant-ing immunity to all Afghans who had fought in the country's civil war, including senior Taliban officials. This was a transparent attempt to shield senior commanders from prosecution for their part in wartime atrocities. It also contradicted the government's *Action Plan for Peace, Reconciliation and Justice in Afghanistan*, which called for the investigation of past crimes and ruled out any prospect of immunity.[15] Opinion surveys since 2002 have consistently shown that the majority of Afghans want commanders held to account for their crimes during the civil war.

The government's strategy of engaging warlords in the political process in order to transform them into politicians or businessmen has largely failed; although many high-profile commanders have begun wearing business suits and speaking the jargon of democrats, they have merely used their positions to expand their power. While some commanders are more legitimate than others, and deserve to be engaged in the political process, the state must take a resolute stand against predatory figures if it is to extend its writ across the country, counter corruption and establish a monopoly on the use of force. An important opportunity to achieve these goals was missed in the immediate post-Taliban period. However, events since have shown that robust government action, backed by international support, could rectify this mistake.

CHAPTER TWO

Spoiler Groups and the Anti-government Insurgency

While the civil war in Afghanistan was fuelled by power-hungry warlords and competing radicalised Islamic groups, the Taliban, with their harsh interpretation of Islam and with the help of foreign funds, managed to impose order and remain at the helm of the state for five years. Once they were ousted, their increased resolve to keep fighting for power, together with their alliances with other radical groups, Afghans and internationalists, has surprised – and keeps surprising – the international community involved in peacekeeping and counter-insurgency operations in Afghanistan.

The political, geostrategic, religious and tribal affiliations of the Taliban movement

Taliban is the plural form of *taleb*, which means 'seeker' (of knowledge) in Arabic and Urdu. It is also used to refer to a student of Islam. The generic name Taliban stems from the Quranic schools, or madrassas, located in Pakistan, mainly in the North-West Frontier Province (NWFP) and Baluchistan, but also in Karachi and Lahore, where poor Afghan refugee children and orphans found a social structure to receive them.[1] An estimated 20,000 madrassas train students in Pakistan today, up from a couple of hundred at independence in 1947. As an essentially Pashtun movement, the Taliban have been rightly accused of 'ethnic parochialism'.[2]

Between 1994 and 1996, the Taliban took over Afghanistan with a speed that surprised many observers. They started with the support of truck-drivers fed up with being constantly taxed and looted on trips between Afghanistan and Pakistan. They then received financial support from Saudi Arabia and the Pakistani ISI, for use as a proxy force and as a source of recruits to fight India in Kashmir. Under the guidance of Mullah Omar – proclaimed in April 1996 '*Amir al-Momineen*' (Commander of the Faithful) – the Taliban were initially welcomed for bringing security after the reign of the warlords. However, they rapidly lost popular support because of their strict interpretation of Islamic law, learned in radical Pakistani madrassas.

Today, the madrassas are not exclusively responsible for recruiting and training jihadist groups, and only a small proportion of these schools propagate messages of hatred. According to one survey, based on interviews with the relatives of deceased jihadists, madrassas are not the main recruiting ground.[3] Instead, fundamentalist mosques, *Tabligh*[4] preachers and friends' networks are used as recruiting tools. It is, however, not known exactly how many madrassas there are in the Federally Administered Tribal Areas (FATA), and what proportion of them are used for enlisting would-be jihadists.

The Muttahida Majlis-e-Amal in Pakistan

In the FATA, the fundamentalist Deobandi line represents the ideology of the bulk of the madrassas.[5] The foremost Pakistani party defending this line is the Jamiat Ulema-i-Islami (JUI or Assembly of Islamic Clerics), one of the six main religious-political parties in Pakistan unified under the banner of the Muttahida Majlis-e-Amal (MMA or United Action Front).[6] The JUI is divided into two factions named for their respective leaders: JUI-S, led by Sami ul-Haq, and JUI-F, led by Fazl ur-Rahman. Sami ul-Haq, who besides being the MMA co-chair also heads the jihadist Deobandi Darul Uloom Haqqania madrassa,[7] openly supports his long-time friends Mullah Omar and Osama bin Laden.[8]

The pro-Taliban MMA is the main Islamist political force in Baluchistan and NWFP. It was created in October 2001 in response to the 'global war on terror', which Pakistan joined following General Pervez Musharraf's order to end all support for the Taliban regime. There is a clear historical parallel between the creation of the MMA and the creation of the Deobandi religious movement as a reaction to British colonial policy, and one which is deeply rooted in the South Asian Muslim consciousness. The ambiguity of the MMA's very creation resides in the fact that, beyond its hatred for Western values, it is also a tacit partner with Musharraf's coalition. Through its open support for the Taliban, the MMA alliance represents a direct challenge to Afghanistan's stability.

The Taliban as a geostrategic apparatus for Pakistan

Since Pakistan's creation as a sovereign state on 14 August 1947, Pakistani planners have been fixated by the notion of strategic depth: the idea that, in any conflict with India, the defence of Pakistan's eastern borders (namely Kashmir) rests on its western borders with Afghanistan. This meant developing Afghanistan as an allied territory to which Pakistani forces could retreat in the event of war. The significance of strategic depth diminished in May 1998, when Pakistan established its own nuclear deterrent. Nonetheless, some elements within the ISI remain convinced of the notion of strategic depth, and continue to play a key role in Afghanistan. The ISI, whose role and power were boosted following the Soviet invasion of Afghanistan in 1979, became the main instrument in bringing the Taliban regime to power.

In September 2001, the fear that the United States might use India as a base from which to launch *Operation Enduring Freedom* was probably instrumental in Musharraf's decision to end support for the Taliban.[9] However, the extent of the president's control over the ISI is unclear, and ISI support for the Taliban insurgency in Afghanistan has continued. In October 2001, ISI head General Mehmud Ahmed was replaced by a less Taliban-friendly figure, Lieutenant-General Ehsanul Haq, but it is conceivable that ISI agents are acting independently on the ground, exploiting old ties established during the jihad against the Soviets.[10] Musharraf claims that the ISI has arrested 680 al-Qaeda 'operatives', although he has also admitted that he has 'seen reports that "some dissidents" and "retired people" who were prominent in ISI between 1979 and 1989 might be helping to leak intelligence to the Taliban'.[11] It is well known that, in exchange for his support for the United States and *Operation Enduring Freedom*, Musharraf negotiated the evacuation from Afghanistan of Pakistani soldiers, military intelligence personnel and ISI-backed jihadists, particularly from Kunduz in December 2001.[12]

Given that military and religious factors are intertwined in Pakistan, it would be wrong to see Musharraf as a Pakistani Mustafa Kemal, a charismatic military figure defending a secularist government in a Muslim society.[13] The army, particularly the ISI, and the religious parties are closely linked, with the latter legitimising the former. Within the ISI, the Pathans (the Pakistani Pashtuns) constitute the majority group. It is not therefore surprising to find retired high-ranking officers such as Lieutenant-General Hamed Gul, the former chief of ISI and a main element in the original empowerment of the Taliban as a military force, still advocating Pakistani support for the Taliban.[14] According to Husain Haqqani, a former adviser to three Pakistani prime ministers: 'The fact is, the ISI does not consider the Taliban as enemies, and US officials are simply bluffing themselves by failing to see that reality'.[15]

Beyond the loss of strategic depth, Pakistan's main fear in Afghanistan is the reconstitution of relations between Kabul and New Delhi. Starting with its support to the Northern Alliance (or United Front) during the war against the Taliban, India has forged excellent ties with Afghanistan, to Pakistan's dismay. Pakistan has repeatedly accused Indian militias and India's intelligence service, the Research and Analysis Wing (RAW), of training several hundred Baluch tribal dissidents (*Ferraris*), and has claimed that Indian commandoes are operating in Pakistan.[16] India has an extensive diplomatic presence in Afghanistan, with consulates in Mazar-i Sharif, Herat, Kandahar and Jalalabad, in addition to the embassy in Kabul.

The border question

Afghanistan's current frontiers took shape in a series of agreements between 1876 and 1907. The main point of contention on the 2,500 kilo-metre Afghan–Pakistani border centres on the 'Durand Line' agreement, signed in 1893 by Sir Mortimer Durand, the British foreign secretary to the government of India, and the Afghan Emir, Abdur Rahman Khan. This boundary between British India and Afghanistan artificially splits the Pashtun tribes into two different countries, a separation that the Pashtuns have never accepted. In 1947, Afghanistan was the only country to vote against Pakistan's admission to the United Nations due to unresolved tensions over the border.

In response to accusations that militants are freely crossing the Durand Line, Musharraf has repeatedly threatened to fence and mine the Afghan border. This proposal, initially presented in 2005,[17] has been rejected by Karzai because it would recognise the border demarcation that Afghanistan disputes, and would institutionalise the separation between Pashtuns. Another strong argument against fencing the border is the proposed use of land mines: Afghanistan is already one of the most mined countries in the world and suffers from one of the highest rates of mine casualties.[18] Despite the massive costs such fencing would incur and its technical complexity, Pakistani Foreign Secretary Riaz Mohammed Khan announced that the project had started in December 2006.[19]

Since 2003, a Tri-Partite Commission (TPC) – with three sub-groups (on intelligence-sharing, border security and improvised explosive devices) – comprising senior military representatives of Pakistan, Afghanistan, the

United States and NATO, has met regularly to discuss infiltration across the border.[20] In early 2007, an Operational Planning Group was added and a joint Pakistan–Afghanistan–NATO Intelligence Center was set up in Kabul to share tactical and strategic intelligence.[21] Despite these mechanisms, however, there have been numerous skirmishes between Pakistani and Afghan forces along the border.

FATA and the peace treaties

The FATA comprise seven Agencies (from north to south, Bajaur, Mohmand, Khyber, Kurram, Orakzai and North and South Waziristan) and four Tribal Areas adjoining the Districts of Peshawar, Kohat, Banu and Dera Ismail Khan. Directly inherited from the British, they retained their semi-autonomous status when Pakistan became independent in 1947. Dubbed Yaghestan (the land of rebellion), the FATA have a long tradition of feudal fighting and resistance dating back to Alexander the Great.[22] Each Agency is headed by a Political Agent, appointed by the government in Islamabad, but these agents exercise little authority.

The Talibanisation of the FATA accelerated following the influx of Taliban and al-Qaeda commanders in November–December 2001. Since then, a series of peace agreements has been concluded between 'tribal representatives' and the Pakistani government. A verbal deal concluded in Shakai, South Waziristan, on 24 April 2004 with Nek Mohammad – a major Taliban leader – established the basic framework for succeeding deals. Nek Mohammad agreed not to attack Pakistani government targets and to register foreigners or expel them from the territories he controlled. After having reneged on the agreement, Nek Mohammad was allegedly killed by a US missile in June 2004.[23]

The second agreement was signed in February 2005 in Sararogha, South Waziristan, by Baitullah Masood, a representative of Mullah Omar.[24] Mullah Dadullah, another leading Afghan Taliban commander, also witnessed the agreement. However, provisions covering the handing over and registration of foreign fighters were not met and the agreement was repudiated by Baitullah shortly afterwards. Another accord was signed at the end of August 2006 by Dr Fakhar Alam Irfan, the North Waziristan Political Agent, and the Utmanzai tribe and ulema (clerics) representing the Taliban.[25] This deal imposed surprisingly harsh conditions on the government, including the release of all fighters in government custody, the return of all confiscated material (including weapons), the restoration of all tribal privileges, the closure of checkpoints and the cessation of military operations in the area. On the Taliban/tribal side, the agreement

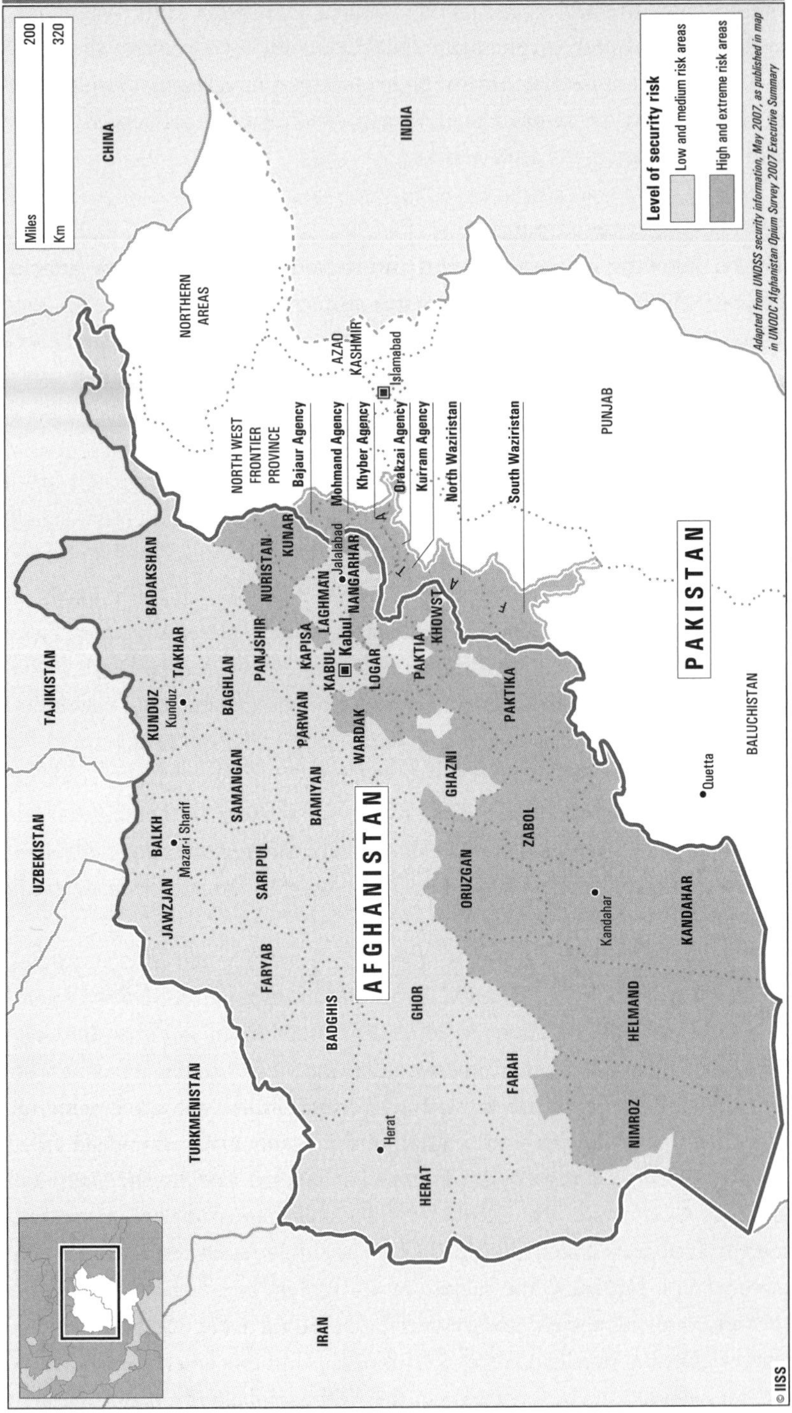

Figure 1: Security risk in Afghanistan and the FATA, May 2007

stipulated that militants stop attacking Pakistani forces and stop crossing the border to attack Coalition and Afghan troops.[26]

Musharraf has defended these arrangements on the grounds that they enable the government to clamp down on foreign elements in the FATA, thereby facilitating the fight against al-Qaeda. Indeed, many foreign fighters (mainly Afghans but also Chechens, Tajiks, Uzbeks, Uighurs and Arab militants) have been handed over to the United States. At the same time, however, these peace agreements have helped to reinforce Taliban safe havens, allowing militants to train and regroup before launching attacks against NATO and Coalition forces in southern Afghanistan.[27]

Beyond the FATA, there is also no doubt that NWFP and Baluchistan have become launching-pads for cross-border attacks in Afghanistan. The former refugee camp of Girdi Jangle, for instance, located 400km from Quetta (the capital of Baluchistan), is a centre of operations for drug- and weapon-trafficking, and appears to act as a Taliban recruitment centre.[28]

'Hot pursuit'

As early as 2002, the question of asserting the right of 'hot pursuit' to follow al-Qaeda and Taliban targets across the border into Pakistan was gaining prominence. In March 2002, Major-General Franklin Hagenbeck of the US 10th Mountain Division noted: 'Hot pursuit would probably be my last resort', and that it would be carried out in coordination with the Pakistani authorities.[29] In June 2004, the United States designated Pakistan a 'Major Non-NATO Ally', a reward for its cooperation and a step that took Islamabad closer to concluding a long-sought-for deal to procure 36 F-16 fighter jets. All the same, Musharraf has not officially authorised US and Coalition forces to carry out hot-pursuit operations into Pakistan. In September 2006, Bush was asked if he thought US forces should use hot pursuit to capture or kill bin Laden and his associates if there was credible evidence that they were based in Pakistan. 'Absolutely', he responded: 'We would take the action necessary to bring them to justice.'[30] However, the question remains taboo within the US military high command, even if US officials sometimes admit that missile strikes launched from *Predator* unmanned aerial vehicles (UAVs) have hit targets in the FATA.[31] Islamabad's position varies between denying that the attacks have taken place, denouncing them as violations of national sovereignty and covering them up as either accidents or Pakistani attacks.[32]

The Central Intelligence Agency (CIA)'s Special Activities (SA) Division has overseen these *Predator* operations, and several successful attacks have been carried out.[33] A January 2006 strike in Damadola (in the Bajaur Agency of the FATA) did not acquire its target, Ayman al-Zawahiri – al-Qaeda's most important figure after bin Laden – but managed to kill senior al-Qaeda members, including Abu Hamza Rabia, an Egyptian field commander, and Haitham al-Yemeni, a Yemeni bomb-maker. *Hellfire* missiles fired from a *Predator* were also responsible for the destruction of a radical madrassa in Chenagai (Bajaur Agency) on 30 October 2006. The madrassa was run by Maulana Liaquat, a senior leader of the banned group *Tehreek-e-Nafaz-e-Shariat-e-Mohammadi* (Movement for the Enforcement of Islamic Laws, TNSM), and allegedly a deputy of al-Zawahiri.

The Kashmir nexus

Indian military officials have repeatedly pointed to the linkage between the Taliban and Kashmiri militants, and have accused the ISI of using Taliban recruits to fight a jihad in Kashmir.[34] The *9/11 Commission Report* also emphasised these connections, citing a US National Security Council memo of October 1998 that warned of 'links between Pakistan's military intelligence service and [Kashmiri radical group] *Harakat-ul-Ansar* trainees at Bin Laden camps near Khowst'.[35]

Two Pakistani groups, Lashkar-e-Taiba (the Army of the Righteous, LeT) and the Deobandi Jaish-e-Mohammed (the Army of Mohammad, JeM), have been at the forefront of the conflict in Indian-administered Kashmir. JeM is also connected to Sipah-e-Sahaba Pakistan (SSP, a violent anti-Shia group) and Lashkar-e-Jhangvi (the Army of Jhangvi – Jhangvi was the founding leader of SSP), which was in turn linked to the killing of 11 French navy technicians in Karachi and the murder of American journalist Daniel Pearl in 2002.[36] The founders of LeT participated in the Afghan jihad against the Soviet Union and had links with Western intelligence agencies.[37] LeT has claimed responsibility for pioneering suicide bombings in India, a type of operation that has become increasingly common in Afghanistan. LeT and JeM both train in the FATA, and have taken part in military operations in southern Afghanistan.[38] The Pakistani government banned both LeT and JeM in 2002, following attacks on the Indian parliament in December 2001. Nonetheless, it would be in line with Pakistan's modus operandi to let JeM and LeT conduct destabilisation operations in Afghanistan. Pakistan derives important benefits from the activities of these groups, as the ongoing conflict in Kashmir ties down around 700,000 Indian troops.

The Tribal Areas have become the jihadist sanctuary that *Operation Enduring Freedom* was supposed to foreclose in Afghanistan. The withdrawal of Pakistani forces into their barracks, after suffering more than 750 casualties since the beginning of their operations in support of OEF, worsened the lawless situation. What the International Crisis Group has dubbed a destabilisation of Afghanistan by Pakistan's 'ambivalent approach and failure to take effective action' only threatens to get worse.[39]

The Taliban's command and control structure

The Afghan and Pakistani Taliban should be viewed within the same framework. It is not accurate to talk about 'neo-Taliban', as the Taliban never disappeared but simply blended into the wider population and regrouped. The Taliban-led insurgency is not a monolith but rather an amalgam of various groups with different motivations, from peasants fighting for a decent wage to madrassa-indoctrinated youths or villagers following the directions of tribal or clan elders. The Taliban command and control structure has greatly benefited from veterans, commanders who fought during the jihad against the Soviets, and younger militants who fought against the Northern Alliance. These elements are referred to by US and NATO forces as 'Tier One Taliban'. They are believed to be more sophisticated in their tactics and better armed than the 'Tier Two Taliban', the locally hired rank-and-file used as ground troops. These fighters can be employed on a 'part-time' basis, and return to their villages after an operation has been staged.

The main command and control hub for the Taliban is in Quetta, the capital of Baluchistan, where the leadership *shura*[40] (council) sits; it is made up of the dozen, mainly Kandahari, Taliban founding members. Besides Mullah Omar, Mullah Qari Abdullah, the former Taliban intelligence chief, and Mullah Baradar Akhund, the former head of the Taliban council in Kabul, are believed to be members of the Quetta *shura*.[41] From the *shura* stem three military commands: one in Quetta, which runs operations in southern Afghanistan (Kandahar, Helmand, Uruzgan and Farah); one in the NWFP capital Peshawar, which runs operations north of the Khyber Pass (in Jalalabad, Kunar, Logar and Laghman); and one in Miran Shah, the capital of North Waziristan, which oversees operations in the eastern provinces of Khost, Paktya and Paktika.[42]

Jalaluddin Haqqani,[43] the former Taliban minister of tribal affairs, who runs several radical madrassas in Waziristan, together with his brother, Haji Khalil, who manages another fundamentalist madrassa in Miran Shah, and his son Sirajuddin Haqqani, play a key role in Waziristan, running what they call the 'Islamic Emirate of Waziristan'. In the FATA, the leadership of the Pakistani Taliban is represented by Haji Omar, a veteran of the Soviet war in Afghanistan, and Baitullah Masood. Other members of the Taliban leadership include Mullah Abdul Khaliq and Mullah Sadiq Noor.[44]

The two main blows US forces have delivered against the Taliban leadership are the killing of Mullah Akhtar Mohammad Osmani in an air strike in December 2006, and the killing of Mullah Dadullah in May 2007 by Afghan and Coalition forces in Helmand. According to Pakistani journalist Ahmed Rashid, Mullah Osmani's death was 'the first casualty among the top Taliban leadership in the past five years'.[45] One Afghan intelligence source states that Osmani was also part of the Quetta *shura*, as was Dadullah, who can be considered the most significant Taliban target to date.[46] In addition to leading Taliban operations in southern Afghanistan, Mullah Dadullah ordered massacres of Shi'ites in 2001 and the murder of a Red Cross expatriate in 2003. He was particularly famous for his combativeness and cruelty,[47] pushing for the beheading of civilians and the recruitment of suicide bombers.

Aside from these two successes, almost all of the top Taliban leadership is still at large. Taliban forces as a whole are estimated at between 7,000 and 12,000 men, according to NATO and Taliban figures.[48] Considering the high casualty rates inflicted by NATO, the Coalition and the ANSF in 2006 – 3,500 of the 4,000 combat-related deaths reported in 2006 were Taliban – it is clear that the movement has had little trouble recruiting new troops.[49]

Jihadist metastasis: conciliating tribalism and internationalist jihad

Beyond the specificity of the Afghan insurgency, the apparent convergence in the international jihadist discourse between Iraq and Afghanistan – the two main 'lands of jihad' – is growing stronger. With the loss of Afghanistan as a central geographical sanctuary,[50] al-Qaeda, the Taliban and Hizb-i Islami have all adapted and merged into several fronts in southern and eastern Afghanistan, even though they differ in their creation and initial goals. Again, the Taliban cannot be understood as a unified movement, and the various motives of the two 'Tiers' range from Pashtun nationalism (for the majority of Taliban) to an internationalist ideology.

The Afghan, or rather Pashtun, nationalist narrative plays on the strong sense of resistance built upon the collective myth of combating foreign forces since the time of Alexander the Great. The British presence in Helmand has revived images of the Anglo-Afghan wars, from the Gandamak massacre in 1842 to tales of Malalai, the Afghan heroine, raising the Afghan flag at the battle of Maiwand in 1880. Then there is the internationalist jihadi narrative, which speaks of a Muslim resistance against foreign troops in a land of Islam, playing on the idea of the umma (the community of believers) and transcending borders. These two narratives mark the strongest division behind the goals and motivations of the Taliban and al-Qaeda.

In order to regain lost ground, the Taliban movement has engaged in what appears to be a systematic campaign of intimidation and killings against tribal elders (*Maleks*) and pro-government figures. Since 2005, around 200 *Maleks* and government officials accused of being 'US spies' have been killed in the FATA, most of them in Waziristan,[51] allowing the Taliban to replace local authorities with radical mullahs. The killing and intimidation of *Maleks* and the emergence of suicide terrorism killings show that the jihadi narrative is rapidly gaining ground within the Afghan insurgency.

Taliban tactics

The ANSF, NATO and the Coalition face an extremely agile enemy employing a wide variety of tactics, from asymmetric attrition warfare to full-scale frontal encounters. Between 2002 and 2006, the Taliban focused primarily on 'soft targets', such as aid workers and government employees.[52] In 2006 and 2007, as the Taliban have gained momentum with the deployment of an increasing number of foreign troops in their southern regional stronghold, they have begun to show greater boldness and have attacked a wider range of targets. Anti-personnel and anti-tank landmines have been laid overnight around US and NATO positions, and rocket attacks have been launched against static positions and moving convoys. The insurgents have also mounted increasingly sophisticated ambushes. 'Baited ambushes', for instance, involve the use of a secondary device, which explodes once rescuers and security forces are on the scene. Improvised explosive devices (IEDs) are the insurgents' most lethal weapon. Between 2005 and 2006, IED attacks more than doubled, from 783 to 1,677.[53] Combining IEDs with suicide vehicles has helped to increase the lethality of attacks. Large-formation frontal assaults, involving hundreds of Taliban troops, have also become more common, as exemplified by the battle of Panjwai in 2006. In the Taliban-dominated border town of Chaman in Baluchistan, adjacent to the Afghan village of Spin Boldak, Taliban fighters are said to cross the Afghan border in waves of 300 motorbikes, queuing and crossing all at the same time.[54]

As with Kashmir, there is a link between the terrorist attacks in Iraq and those conducted in Afghanistan. For instance, following the Iraqi example, coerced suicide bombings, where the bomber's family is threatened if he does not conduct his mission, have been documented in Afghanistan.[55] Suicide attacks – unknown in Afghanistan's previous wars – are the hallmark of al-Qaeda, which launched the first such attack in Afghanistan with the assassination of the Northern Alliance leader Ahmad Shah Massoud on 9 September 2001. Since then, the number of suicide attacks has risen sharply, reaching 139 in 2006.[56] Calls for jihad and martyrdom, threats, promises of monetary compensation and strict indoctrination have all fed the growing stream of volunteers. Recruitment is typically done in NWFP or Baluchistan, and involves the most senior Taliban (a video showing Mullah Dadullah, the late Taliban commander, enlisting would-be martyrs can be found on the video-sharing website YouTube).[57] Suicide bombings vary in their form, from a man carrying a bag full of explosives in a bus or wearing an explosive jacket in a crowd, to bicycle riders carrying explosive charges or militants driving suicide vehicles (cars and trucks). The lethality of these attacks is also increasing as suicide bombers, professionally trained by seasoned al-Qaeda militants, learn from the failures of their predecessors.

The Taliban also often run improvised checkpoints on secondary roads in the south, and have seized control of government district centres or isolated police stations, holding them for a few weeks before melting away. Civilians, particularly women and children, are increasingly used as human shields. Beyond the obvious propaganda advantage that accrues from civilian casualties of NATO fire – the Taliban maintained a website dedicated to this issue[58] – this tactic may be designed to compel NATO forces to engage in more close-combat operations.

Abductions, which have a long history in Afghanistan, are increasingly used as a tactic, targeting international contractors and aid workers, not only to pass on a political message and attract media attention but also to secure substantial gains such as alleged cash rewards and the liberation of key Taliban commanders. One of the most notorious cases was the release of Mullah Dadullah's brother, Mullah Shah Mansoor, and four Taliban fighters in exchange for the release of an Italian journalist kidnapped in March 2007. Even though surveillance operations following Mansoor's release have allowed the killing of Dadullah by a squadron of Britain's Special Boat Service (SBS),[59] the incident was part of a dangerous series of hostage negotiations involving hostages' home countries (France, Italy, South Korea, China, Germany and others) in the negotiation process.

Jihadist propaganda

Jihadist publications are readily available in Peshawar and Quetta, and their study helps us to understand the mind of the jihadists. These publications include *Talaa-i-Khorasan* (*The Vanguard of Khorasan* – the name comes from the early caliphate created at the end of the Persian Sassanid Empire, which encompassed most of Central Asia), *Tora Bora*, *Estiqamat* and Gulbuddin Hekmatyar's weekly magazine *Tanweer*. The first two magazines are international in character, published in Arabic with articles translated from Pashtu. The Taliban distribute these magazines, along with other leaflets, among the Pashtun population on both sides of the border. In addition, up to 70 radio stations broadcast extremist propaganda in the Tribal Areas, taking advantage of a powerful medium that is easily accessible and appreciated by Afghans.[60] *Talaa-i-Khorasan* and *Tora Bora* are also published in PDF format on the Internet, as is a wealth of other material, including online magazines, chat rooms, forums, bulletin boards and news groups.[61] Al-Qaeda's Pakistan-based As Sahaab (The Clouds) Foundation edits and produces cheap VCDs and DVDs depicting the recruitment of suicide bombers, IED attacks and the killing of 'American spies'. Meanwhile, Taliban figures make appearances on media outlets ranging from al-Jazeera to the British Broadcasting Corporation (BBC).

An exhaustive analysis of the insurgency's discourse can help shed light on the evolution of the jihadist movement in Afghanistan. Although textual analysis has its limitations – wartime communication being part information, part propaganda – discourse analysis offers an insight into the insurgent groups, highlighting the themes they use to mobilise fighters and legitimise their actions. Research laboratories like the Radicalization Watch Project located in Saint-Cyr, the French Military Academy, are reviewing available communications, focusing exclusively on groups that have claimed responsibility for armed attacks in Afghanistan.[62] Their conclusions are:

- that the Afghanistan discourse is increasingly dominated by references to the achievements and field techniques of the Iraqi insurgency;
- that there is a gradual convergence around common practices and discourse;
- that there is a growing awareness of public opinion, and groups are increasingly mindful of their image; and
- that, unlike the Iraqi groups, Afghan militants have a clear political programme and a long-term vision for Afghanistan.

The traditional theme of the clash between Islam and the West is reinforced in al-Qaeda's propaganda, which claims that Afghanistan has been invaded once again, this time by the 'crusaders and the Jews'. Extremist propaganda exploits the language and imagery of the 'clash of civilisations' to promote this notion and attract new adherents.

Taliban PSYOPS

Psychological Operations (PSYOPS) are 'planned operations to convey selected information … to influence [an audience's] emotions, motives, objective reasoning, and ultimately the behaviour of governments, organizations, groups, and individuals'.[63] *Shab-nama* ('night letters') are one of the most effective PSYOPS techniques used by the Taliban. These letters, which were also used against Soviet occupying forces and their collaborators, carry threats typically aimed at schoolteachers, pro-government clerics, health workers and government employees, promising death to anyone who works for 'the infidels'. One of the main purposes of these letters is to dissuade Afghans from providing intelligence on Taliban insurgents to the government or international forces. The threats detailed in these letters have been carried out with increasing ferocity. In 2006, scores of schools were burned down; coupled with escalating levels of violence more generally, this kept an estimated 100,000 students out of school.[64] Night letters have also been used to warn poppy farmers against obeying the government's ban on cultivation.

Gulbuddin Hekmatyar's Hizb-i Islami (Party of Islam)

Gulbuddin Hekmatyar is a Kharoty Pashtun from the Ghilzai tribal group.[65] During the jihad against the Soviet Union, he headed one of the seven Sunni resistance groups supported by Pakistan and America, the so-called 'Peshawar 7'.[66] Founded in 1975 in Pakistan, the Hizb-i Islami grew out of Hekmatyar's initial affiliation with the Muslim Brotherhood. Although one of the best-funded and most effective mujahadeen commanders in the US-supported anti-Soviet war, Hekmatyar was also a staunch anti-Western fundamentalist. The Hizb-i Islami maintained close links with the ISI, and was in fact the mirror party of Jamaat-i Islami (JI) in Pakistan (now part of the MMA). Although appointed Afghan prime minister in 1993, Hekmatyar was a principal combatant in the intra-mujahadeen struggle between 1993 and 1996. The Hizb-i Islami militia was responsible for much of the destruction suffered by Kabul, the main battle ground, and for many of the more than 50,000 civilian casualties.

In 2001, Hekmatyar threw his support behind the Taliban. Hizb-i Islami Gulbuddin (HIG) insurgent activity has been centred on Laghman, Nangahar and Logar, and in Hekmatyar's traditional strongholds of Paktya, Khost and Kunar. In May 2006, in a video sent to al-Jazeera, Hekmatyar declared that he was ready to fight 'under the banner of al-Qaeda'.[67] Even though Hekmatyar's relationship with the Taliban has traditionally been problematic, together with the Taliban and al-Qaeda HIG represents one of the three corners of the 'terror triangle' in Afghanistan.[68]

Al-Qaeda: still there

Since its resistance against the Soviet invasion of 1979, Afghanistan has enjoyed a special place at the pinnacle of Muslim collective conscious-ness. Well aware of this, bin Laden wrote in 2000: 'It is compulsory upon all Muslims all over the world to help Afghanistan. And to make *hijra* [migrate] to this land, because it is from this land that we will dispatch our armies all over the world to smash all *kuffar* [non-believers] all over the world'.[69]

Contrary to the commonly held view that al-Qaeda has become merely an idea or a brand-name, it is still extremely active in Afghanistan, and the rise of suicide attacks there bears the hallmarks of al-Qaeda's tactics. It has also demonstrated the efficiency of its alliance with HIG and the Taliban. In December 2001, bin Laden and al-Qaeda, with a group of 200 Saudis and Yemenis, escaped to Parachinar[70] (the capital of Kurram Agency in the FATA), next to Tora Bora, with help from the Afghan commander Anwar ul Haq Mujahed.[71] The case of Tahir Yuldash is a relevant example of the nexus between al-Qaeda and the Taliban. Yuldash was a deputy to the leader of the Islamic Movement of Uzbekistan (IMU, closely linked to al-Qaeda), Juma Namangani, until Namangani was killed in Afghanistan in a US air strike in October 2001. Mullah Omar reportedly appointed Yuldash commander-in-chief of Taliban forces in Afghanistan's northern provinces, with command of the remnants of Tajik and Uzbek militants there.[72]

Around 1,500 foreign fighters (Tajiks, Uzbeks, Chechens, Kazakhs, Uighurs and Arabs) are believed to be in the FATA,[73] although these numbers vary as they are constantly moving backwards and forwards across the border. Besides Kashmiri groups, such as the Harakat-ul-Mujahideen (HuM), many non-Afghan affiliates of al-Qaeda, such as the IMU, Ansar-al-Islam and Chechen groups, have long-standing connec-tions with Afghanistan, and have waged operations and exchanged tactics and techniques between their home bases and Afghanistan, via al-Qaeda. According to British and US intelligence, 100 of al-Qaeda's most expe-rienced operatives[74] (part of NATO's 'Tier One' classification) are now leading Taliban attacks within Afghanistan.

To complete this picture we must also point to the TNSM. This ultraviolent Pakistani jihadist movement, close to al-Qaeda and known as the 'Black Turbans', was created in 1989 and banned in January 2002 by Musharraf. With its base in Malakand (northern NWFP), the TNSM is operating from Peshawar and the Bajaur Agency.[75] The TNSM uses its strong historical networks in Afghanistan to conduct cross-border operations with the Hizb-i Islami, as the TNSM founder, Sufi Mohammad, was a JI militant close to Hekmatyar.

Friendly fundamentalists?

On the advice of former US presidential envoy and Ambassador to Afghanistan Zalmay Khalilzad, Karzai has followed an open-handed policy towards the fundamentalists, both within and outside the regime. The rationale behind this approach was to separate moderates from radicals, marginalising the former and bringing the latter under the umbrella of the state. The first target of this policy was the Hizb-i Islami, which Karzai tried to rally to his side (with very little success) by asking its members to join a democratic Afghanistan and reject Hekmatyar's radical vision of Islam.

When it was created, the Afghan government already had Islamist members. One notable example is Abdul Rabb Rasul Sayyaf, founder of the Ittihad-i Islami (Islamic Union) and a close ally of Karzai. Sayyaf is a Pashtun Wahhabist fundamentalist, with close ties to Saudi Arabia, where he spent a number of years. At one time he was also very close to bin Laden. Sayyaf is as responsible as Hekmatyar for the destruction and killings in Kabul between 1992 and 1996. He is also mentioned in the *9/11 Commission Report*, in its section on 'Terrorist Entrepreneurs'. Abu Sayyaf, the main Islamist militant group in the Philippines, was named after him, and its founder, Abdurajak Janjalani, was a student of Sayyaf's. Sayyaf is now a 'respectable' figure, and a member of parliament with the ear of Karzai.[76]

Following the September 2005 parliamentary elections, the Wolesi Jirga (Lower House) now has up to 34 MPs officially registered as members of Hizb-i Islami.[77] They are led by Khalid Farooqi, a Hizb-i Islami mujahadeen commander in Paktika during the war against the Soviets. Although they have reportedly severed all ties with Gulbuddin Hekmatyar, many suspect that links remain. Four prominent members of the Taliban regime also won seats in parliament, including former Talib Governor Abdul Salaam 'Rocketi' (his nickname stems from his dexterity at shooting RPG-7s at Soviet tanks during the jihad).

Iran's role

Besides the fact that both countries share a common language, historical and socio-cultural factors are vital to understanding Iran's role in Afghanistan: Herat and Kandahar were part of the Persian Empire until 1747.

Iran's role in the security sector in Afghanistan is ambiguous. On the one hand, concerns over the return of the Taliban and the export of drugs to Iran have meant that Tehran has been very supportive of the Karzai regime. On the other hand, Iran is concerned over the long-term presence of US forces, and so maintains links with Hazara Shia groups.[78] The Taliban, following a Wahhabist version of Islam in which Shi'ites are considered deviants and sinners, carried out atrocities against the Hazaras, including mass murders and child rapes (mainly of boys). Iran welcomed the outcome of the US intervention in 2001 to the extent that it allowed the repatriation of over two million of the more than three million Afghan refugees residing in Iran, and removed an antagonistic regime. Moreover, Iran, which has several million heroin addicts, has been keen to see the consolidation of an Afghan regime capable of containing the opium trade.

In January 2002, Tehran pledged $560m over five years at the Tokyo donors' conference. Since then, Iran has worked assiduously to advance its influence in Afghanistan through the provision of aid and the development of commercial links. Initiatives supported by Tehran include the renovation and refurbishment of hospitals, the construction of a 110-kilometre road – by far the best in Afghanistan – connecting Herat with the Iranian border, and the installation of customs posts. Iran is also planning a railway project to link the two countries, and is working on a scheme to facilitate Afghan access to the port of Chabahar.

Iran still has the potential, through its various proxies and its alleged financial support to newly elected Afghan MPs,[79] to be a destabilising power if it chooses. From the Iranian perspective, the US presence close to Iran, particularly at Shindand airbase, which is just 100km from the Iranian border, is a source of concern. A shipment of Iranian-made weapons was intercepted in the Kandahar region in early 2007, and in June 2007 Nicholas Burns, the US under secretary of state for political affairs, claimed that 'there's irrefutable evidence the Iranians are now doing this [transferring weapons to the Taliban] and it's a pattern of activity'.[80] Among weapons of Iranian origin found in Afghanistan, armour-piercing Explosive-Formed Projectiles (EFPs) are of particular concern. EFPs are allegedly supplied by the Iranian Islamic Revolutionary Guard Corps (IRGC) and its Quds Force elite unit to Shia insurgents in Iraq.[81] They first appeared in areas of Afghanistan close to the Iranian border in April 2007.[82]

CHAPTER THREE

The Opium Trade

An overview of the opium trade

Opium cultivation is at the heart of the Afghan security problem. It is intertwined with issues of governance, corruption, warlordism and the Taliban-led insurgency. The figures are staggering. In 2007, Afghanistan produced a record 8,200 metric tonnes of opium, twice the total amount of 2005, with a farm-gate value equivalent to 13% of Afghanistan's official gross domestic product (GDP) and accounting for 93% of all the world's heroin.[1] Since 1991, Afghanistan has been the world's main opium producer, surpassing Myanmar.[2] In no other country in the world has illegal narcotics represented such a massive share of the domestic economy. Billions of dollars have been spent on counter-narcotics operations – encompassing interdiction, eradication, public information and alternative-livelihood programmes – and the mainstreaming of counter-narcotics in the Afghan reconstruction project has meant that a large percentage of donor-funded projects have a counter-narcotics element. Any effective response to the poppy boom must feature an integrated and nationwide approach in order to avoid merely displacing production from one region to another. As with the insurgency, security forces – in this case specialised counter-narcotics police – are necessary but far from sufficient to contain the problem.

In July 2000, Mullah Omar issued an edict declaring opium *haram* (un-Islamic) – by far the most effective measure against poppy cultivation ever taken in Afghanistan. Following the ban, total Afghan opium production fell to 185 tonnes, and production was mainly confined to the northern

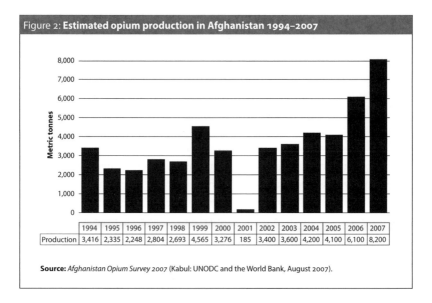

Figure 2: **Estimated opium production in Afghanistan 1994–2007**

	1994	1995	1996	1997	1998	1999	2000	2001	2002	2003	2004	2005	2006	2007
Production	3,416	2,335	2,248	2,804	2,693	4,565	3,276	185	3,400	3,600	4,200	4,100	6,100	8,200

Source: *Afghanistan Opium Survey 2007* (Kabul: UNODC and the World Bank, August 2007).

province of Badakhshan, which was controlled by the Northern Alliance.[3] The farm-gate price was then around $30/kg. A year after the ban, prices had reached $700/kg thanks to the resultant shortage. Following this brief interlude, however, opium production has resumed the upward trend that began in the 1980s.

Incidentally, the quality and purity of Afghan heroin have steadily improved; whereas in the 1980s production yielded mainly 'brown sugar' (lower-grade heroin), Afghanistan now produces high-grade 'china white', with levels of heroin chlorhydrate up to 98%.[4] In addition, due to the high morphine content of the opium poppies (*Papaver somniferum*) grown in Afghanistan, only 6kg or 7kg of opium – instead of the typical 10kg – is required to produce 1kg of heroin. While over-production has contributed to a decline in prices, the higher quality of the opium is leading to higher addiction rates among consumers. A new, highly addictive drug found in Iran, called 'compressed heroin', uses 20kg of opium to produce 1kg.[5]

Of the estimated $2.7bn export value of the drug trade, after unofficial taxes to warlords, local authorities and/or Taliban militants, only around $500m actually benefits farmers. This is equivalent to less than 2% of the profits from the global heroin trade, estimated at $30bn in 2005. Some 509,000 households are involved at the production stage, with 3.3m Afghans directly benefiting from cultivation. Then there are the indirect benefits to the Afghan economy; there is little doubt, for instance, that opium money has helped the Afghan currency, the afghani, to remain stable since its revaluation in 2002.

The major reasons for planting this illicit crop used to be survival, debt[6] and quick profits. The traditional Afghan practice of money-lending in the agricultural sector is the *salaam*, a form of micro-credit with high interest rates, involving a monetary advance on expected future crop production, usually contracted at the beginning of the season and paid at the harvest. As Jonathan Goodhand underlines, this system places the debt-laden farmer in a patron–client relationship with the lender, who is usually a local trader.[7] Another factor pushing peasants to cultivate opium, particularly in southern Afghanistan, are the night letters issued either by the Taliban or by local commanders who benefit from the production and trafficking of opium. There is also direct intimidation, in the form of threats of retaliation if cultivation is discontinued.[8] However, as poppy production continues unabated in southern Afghanistan, greed and corruption are becoming major motives for cultivation.

Who precisely benefits from the opium trade is unclear. Antonio Maria Costa, the head of the United Nations Office on Drugs and Crime (UNODC), has accused Sher Mohammad Akhundzada, the former governor of Helmand Province, of encouraging farmers to grow poppies before he was removed from office in December 2005 (there was a 162% rise in cultivation in Helmand, the largest producing province, accounting for 50% of the entire Afghan poppy crop in 2007).[9] The Akhundzada family has long been involved in the opium trade; in the 1980s, Nassim Akhundzada's[10] trafficking network competed with Hizb-i Islami networks. Nassim was assassinated in 1990, whereupon his brother Ghulam Rassoul took over the network before he too was killed. Sher Muhammad, Ghulam Rassoul's son, was nominated by Karzai as Helmand's governor, and then later appointed to the Senate. One of Karzai's brothers, Ahmed Wali Karzai, is regularly accused by various sources within the international community and by former Afghan government officials of being heavily involved in the drug trade.

The structure of the trade

Heroin/morphine processing is increasingly carried out in Afghanistan, mainly because of the monetary value it adds and also for export and storage convenience. Reaching the first transformation stage (leading to morphine base) is fairly easy, and allows for a 90% reduction in the weight of the product. Over the past ten years, the ratio of opium to heroin or morphine exports has reversed, from 3:1 to 1:3. The Afghan government has been pressed to target processing laboratories, but this is not an easy task, as they can operate virtually anywhere, using a few metal drums and a press. In order to finalise the production process, quantities of acetic anhydride and other chemical agents are needed. Tracking imports of these precursors is one way of locating processing laboratories, although this is also difficult as smuggling routes are numerous.

There is no cartelisation of the Afghan market because the dispersed nature of production means that there is no vertical integration. Nevertheless, consolidation seems to be occurring, as fewer high-level traffickers are being tracked down and identified[11] by counter-narcotics officials in Kabul. In Helmand, the UNODC estimates that there are 1,000–1,500 small opium traders and 300–500 larger traders.[12] However, counter-narcotics officials believe that just 20 to 40 large traffickers control the bulk of the drug traffic in Afghanistan, along with a few hundred mid-level traffickers operating between them and the farmers.[13] Because of the huge volumes being traded in the Kandahar–Helmand market, the strongest drug tycoons have their base in these provinces, with very solid links to Dubai, through which the bulk of Afghan drug money is believed to transit.

Trafficking routes

The main transit route (and a major destination) for the export of Afghan opiates remains via Iran. This is logical, as Iran has the highest per-capita number of heroin addicts in the world, with two million officially recognised by the Iranian government.[14] Over 60% of Afghan opiates still transit (with a large part consumed in) Iran, mainly via the southern Iranian Baluch areas. Tehran has placed great emphasis on interdiction, and has lost almost 3,000 border guards in counter-narcotics operations over the past 20 years. Yet the billion dollars Iran has invested in interdiction efforts, coupled with the stringent penalties meted out to traffickers, with an estimated 10,000 executed over the past two decades, have not stemmed the flow of drugs. A high-ranking counter-narcotics official[15] based in Kabul pointed to the suspected complicity of elements of the Iranian security forces, mainly the Pasdaran or IRGC, in securing the transit of large quantities of drugs through Iranian territory.

To the east, Pakistan, home to close to a million heroin addicts, is the second-busiest transit route for traffickers. The main transit cities are Quetta, Karachi and Peshawar.[16] It is estimated that a large proportion of the drugs crossing Baluchistan actually find their way to Iran. The FATA has traditionally been a transit and processing area for the opium trade, with its access to the ocean via Karachi and Gwadar and its land routes to Central Asia. Besides the existing trafficking networks of the tribal areas,

Taliban control of the region allows safe passage. In northern Afghanistan, opium from Badakhshan usually exits through neighbouring Tajikistan on its way to Russia. Consumption is growing along transit routes as markets become more organised and addiction increases. After Iran and Pakistan, Europe – particularly Italy, Spain and the UK – is the main market.

Corruption

The narcotics trade has been a major source of corruption in the ANSF. Police-chief posts in poppy-growing districts are often awarded through a bidding process, with prices reaching as high as $100,000 for a six-month appointment to a position with a monthly salary of $60.[17] In the highway police – disbanded in 2006 because of massive rates of corruption – mid-level positions were bought for up to $25,000.[18] Such positions entitle officers to large bribes from smugglers in return for protection by the police and even the use of police vehicles. With one exception, no senior Interior Ministry or police official had been prosecuted for involvement in the drug trade by late 2006. The exception, Lieutenant-Colonel Nadir Khan, was sentenced to ten years in prison for stealing and selling 50kg of confiscated heroin.[19]

The involvement of spoiler groups in the drug trade

The involvement of the Taliban in the narcotics trade has gradually increased, particularly in the south. Before their ban on poppy cultivation, the Taliban applied so-called 'Islamic taxes' on opium of up to 20%;[20] other taxes were added during the processing and trafficking stages. Today's drugs are taxed in a similar way. A 'traditional' levy of 10% is paid by farmers to Taliban or militia commanders, depending on who wields the most authority in a particular region. Laboratories pay up to 15% of their revenues, and there is an average transit fee of 15%.[21] According to former Interior Minister Ali Jalali: 'the Taliban encourage poppy production to defy the government and to win the hearts and minds of the population. The drug traffickers also need protection, and typically pay 18–20% of their revenues to the Taliban to cement an alliance of convenience'.[22]

The counter-narcotics campaign

The UK took responsibility as lead nation for counter-narcotics in 2002 under the auspices of the SSR process, and has experimented with several counter-narcotics approaches. In 2002, it launched a controversial money-for-eradication scheme inspired by ex-Finance Minister Ashraf Ghani, then an adviser to Karzai.[23] Farmers were offered a lump sum of $350 per *jerib* (a fifth of a hectare) of poppy field destroyed. With a harvest of 3,600 tonnes the following year, this measure clearly failed; indeed, there is evidence that the cash sum actually acted as an incentive to grow more poppy. The majority of farmers in the south did not receive the promised remuneration, and large amounts of money allocated for the programme were never adequately accounted for. In all, the scheme ended up costing over $100,000 per hectare of poppy destroyed.[24] Since this initial failure, a more hands-on approach has been promoted, targeting laboratories and focusing on law-enforcement training and interdiction efforts on the one hand, and promoting comprehensive rural development and alternative-livelihood programmes on the other. In 2002, the UK led *Operation Headstrong*,[25] an attempt to bolster anti-narcotics efforts by creating and training a 200-strong paramilitary Afghan Special Narcotics Force.

The US role in counter-narcotics has also dramatically increased. In 2004, the US Drug Enforcement Administration (DEA) and the Department of Defense announced their involvement in the 'Kabul Counter-Narcotics Implementation Plan'. The DEA has since deployed Foreign Advisory and Support Teams (FAST) to Afghanistan and has permanently stationed Special Agents and Intelligence Analysts to assist Afghan counter-narcotics officers in their interdiction efforts. As part of the US-led *Operation Containment*, conceived in February 2002, FAST teams[26] conducted investigations aimed at dismantling drug-trafficking and money-laundering organisations, without which several noteworthy opium and heroin seizures in Afghanistan would not have been possible. The US counter-narcotics strategy features five pillars: public information, alternative livelihoods, eradication, interdiction and law enforcement/justice reform. These five elements come from the Afghan government's eight-pillar approach, encapsulated in the Afghan National Drugs Control Strategy[27] launched during the 2006 London donor conference. The UK and other donors involved in counter-narcotics programming contribute to the other three pillars (public awareness, demand reduction and institution-building).

Afghan counter-narcotics institutions

Within the Interior Ministry, the Counter-Narcotics Police of Afghanistan (CNPA) is the leading Afghan agency for law enforcement and interdiction of drugs. The CNPA is trained and mentored by US, UK, German and Norwegian police officers and customs officials. It includes a National Interdiction Unit (NIU), comprising five teams of 25 members each. These units, trained by the US private security company Blackwater, have received advanced instruction in firearms, raid execution, evidence collection and arresting and interviewing techniques. FAST teams also provide support to the NIU.[28]

A Counter-Narcotics Criminal Justice Task Force (CJTF) was established in May 2005, comprising judges, prosecutors, investigators and lawyers specialising in narcotics cases. The CJTF cases are transmitted for prosecution to the Central Narcotics Tribunal (CNT), a dedicated court of 14 judges[29] located in Kabul, with exclusive jurisdiction over major drug cases. The CJTF and CNT relocated in 2007 to a Counter Narcotics Justice Centre, a secure facility equipped with courtrooms and a pre-trial detention centre. A dedicated maximum-security unit has been built within the Pul-i Charkhi prison on the outskirts of Kabul, to detain high-profile drug dealers, but it 'still awaits major drug dealers – rather than drivers and couriers', in UNODC's own words.[30] According to the Interior Ministry, 700 traffickers were arrested during 2006; 420 heroin laboratories were destroyed and 100 tonnes of opium seized.[31] The US was directly involved in two high-profile arrests of major drug traffickers. The first occurred in April 2005, when Haji Bashir Noorzai,[32] a well-known Afghan drug baron, was arrested in New York and charged with smuggling heroin worth $50m into the United States. The following October, another notorious trafficker, Baz Mohammad,[33] was extradited to the US on charges of conspiring to smuggle more than $25m-worth of heroin into the country.

On the policy front, the Counter Narcotics Directorate, formed in October 2002, was upgraded by a presidential decree in December 2004, to become the Ministry of Counter Narcotics. Its role is to coordinate and oversee Afghanistan's counter-narcotics policies, and to monitor and evaluate their implementation. Finally, on the financial side, the United Nations Development Programme (UNDP) established a Counter Narcotics Trust Fund in October 2005 to improve the coordination of donor resources and expenditures.

The eradication dilemma

Eradication has been one of the most contentious elements of counter-narcotics strategy. Many have argued that eradication without an integrated approach to development would only lead to the further impoverishment of Afghan farmers. In a 2005 report on Afghanistan, UNODC warned that 'eradicated fields leave families in economic distress, trigger humanitarian disaster, and increase the temptation to join the insurgency'.[34]

In May 2004, the Interior Ministry launched a 700-strong Central Poppy Eradication Force (CPEF). The CPEF is supported by the US State

Department and trained by DynCorp, a US private security company which also conducts eradication missions in Colombia. Simultaneously, an eradication programme began, in which provincial governors were given funds to advance eradication. The programme was heavily criticised on the grounds that governors were targeting rivals, while leaving their allies unmolested. Independently of the CPEF, US-backed Poppy Elimination Program (PEP) teams are working in seven provinces (Kandahar, Nangarhar, Uruzgan, Farah, Badakhshan, Helmand and Balkh) to monitor and evaluate eradication efforts, reporting to the minister of counter-narcotics.

Aerial spraying has proved controversial, and has not been pursued. However, in December 2006 John Walters, the Director of the US Office of National Drug Control Policy, announced that Afghan poppies would be sprayed with glyphosate herbicides.[35] Meanwhile, the Senlis Council, a non-governmental organisation, has proposed a licencing system covering opiates used to make licit painkillers such as morphine.[36] The proposal – based on the false assumption of a global shortage of morphine[37] – is, however, unworkable as it would be impossible to control licit opium production in a country where the rule of law has barely reached beyond the main cities. As the former Afghan minister of counter narcotics, Habibullah Qaderi, pointed out: 'There is no control mechanism to force farmers to sell the opium they produce to manufacture medicines rather than to drug-traffickers'.[38] Even if it could be done, the average price of pharmaceutical opiates is far lower than the illicit-market price, so farmers would still gravitate towards the illicit market. The plan is also danger-ous as it sends a contradictory message to Afghan farmers, undermining public-awareness campaigns against poppy cultivation undertaken by the Afghan government and the international community.[39]

Part 2: **Combating the Threats to Afghanistan's Security**

CHAPTER FOUR

International Military Support

Operation Enduring Freedom

On 21 September 2001, ten days after the attacks on the United States, General Tommy Franks, head of US Central Command (CENTCOM), proposed to Bush that 'US Central Command, as a part of America's Global War on Terrorism … would destroy the Al Qaeda network inside Afghanistan along with the illegitimate Taliban regime which was harbouring and protecting the terrorists'.[1] Two weeks later, on 7 October, *Operation Enduring Freedom* (OEF)[2] was launched. In the initial phase, long-range US bombers (B1s, B2s and B52s) were used extensively, together with F-14 and F-18 carrier-based fighters. In parallel, *Tomahawk* cruise missiles were launched from US and British platforms. On 13 November 2001, in defiance of US requests to stay out of the capital until American forces arrived, the Northern Alliance seized Kabul and Jalalabad.

One of the main battlegrounds in the first phase of OEF was Tora Bora, in Afghanistan's eastern Nangarhar province. Following the successful use of airpower in the Balkans, the US and other Western countries had been seduced by what Sir Lawrence Freedman calls 'the temptation of air power' and its prospect of 'zero casualties'.[3] As a result, insufficient troops were deployed on the ground at this early stage, and bin Laden and the rest of the al-Qaeda leadership was allowed to escape. According to Gary Bernsten, a former CIA Clandestine Service field commander in Tora Bora: 'The biggest and most important failure of CENTCOM leadership came at Tora Bora when they turned down my request for a battalion of US Rangers to block bin Laden's escape'.[4]

Since the failure at Tora Bora, the Coalition has conducted numerous operations in Afghanistan. The first major offensive, *Operation Anaconda*, took place in March 2002 in the mountains south of Gardez in Paktya province. Its aim was to destroy remaining pockets of al-Qaeda and Taliban resistance. By then, al-Qaeda and the Taliban had adapted to US precision air strikes, and were 'practicing systematic communications security, dispersal, camouflage discipline, use of cover and concealment'.[5] Although hundreds of enemy combatants were declared killed, only 30 bodies were recovered.

Four years after *Anaconda*, major military operations gathered momentum again; *Operation Medusa* was launched in September 2006 in Panjwai district, 35km south of Kandahar. Led by Canada, the operation saw the highest enemy combatant casualty toll ever inflicted by NATO ground troops. According to General James Jones, then NATO's Supreme Allied Commander in Europe, between 1,000 and 1,500 Taliban fighters were killed. Before the operation was launched, leaflets were air-dropped asking the population to evacuate, and tribal leaders were consulted on how to conduct the evacuations. A second Canadian-led operation, *Baaz Tsuka* (*Falcon Summit*), was launched in Panjwai in December 2006. Another operation, *Mountain Fury* in September 2006, focused on the border provinces of Paktika, Khost and Paktya, as well as Ghazni and Logar. It was conducted by Coalition troops and the ANSF. British and Canadian military analysts have described the fighting their armies faced in southern Afghanistan in 2006 as the fiercest they have encountered since the Korean War in the 1950s. In 2007, following *Operation Volcano* (January–February) in the north of Kajaki, the main NATO operation was *Operation Achilles* in Helmand province, where more than 4,500 ISAF troops and 1,000 ANSF soldiers conducted a sweeping offensive after British Royal Marines cleared the Taliban stronghold around the Kajaki dam. *Operation Hammer* (2,000 ISAF and ANSF soldiers, including 1,500 British troops) began in July 2007, to drive the Taliban out of the Gereshk valley in Helmand.

From the beginning of the war, air power has played an indispensable role in all Coalition operations; its importance in the Afghan theatre is particularly evident due to the rugged and inhospitable topography of the country, and the limited number of combat troops available for operations. Munitions used include the 15,000lb BLU-82 'daisy cutter', deployed in the Tora Bora battle of December 2001, and 5,000lb GBU-28 bombs, which were primarily developed to penetrate hardened bunkers. AGM-130 air-to-surface missiles were used to seal caves in and around Tora Bora.[6] The new BLU-118/B thermobaric bomb was dropped on a cave in Gardez in March 2002, amid controversial talk in the United States of reviving tactical nuclear weapons programmes to attack hard and deeply buried targets.

ISAF and NATO

ISAF was established on 20 December 2001, under UN Security Council Resolution 1386, with an initial six-month mandate. The mission was authorised to use force under Chapter VII of the UN Charter, and was given 'complete and unimpeded freedom of movement throughout the territory and airspace of Afghanistan'.[7] ISAF was tasked with helping the Afghan Interim Authority to develop national-security structures, assist in the development and training of the newly formed Afghan security forces and support the country's reconstruction. By 2007, ISAF comprised troops from 37 nations, including all 26 NATO member states.

On 11 August 2003, NATO assumed authority for the ISAF mission, beginning a four-stage geographical expansion beyond the initial focus on Kabul. The staged expansion came to an end in October 2006, when NATO assumed overall responsibility for security in all regions of the country. Of the 23,000 US troops operating in Afghanistan, 12,000 were placed under NATO command, bringing the total number of ISAF troops to 31,000. The remaining 11,000 US troops continue to conduct counter-insurgency operations under the auspices of Coalition Joint Task Force (CJTF)-76, with its headquarters at Bagram airbase outside Kabul (CJTF-76 also acts as a de facto HQ for ISAF's Regional Command (RC) East). Beyond ISAF HQ in Kabul (RC Capital), ISAF's other Regional Commands are RC North, under Germany, RC West, led by Italy, and RC South, led by the UK.

NATO's mission in Afghanistan comprises five phases:

- Phase 1: Assessment and Preparation, including operations in Kabul (completed).
- Phase 2: Geographic Expansion (completed).
- Phase 3: Stabilisation.
- Phase 4/5: Transition/Redeployment.

NATO's arrival in the unstable south saw it shift towards direct counter-insurgency operations, while at the same time trying to maintain a reconstruction focus. Helmand had hosted a small US contingent (130 troops at its maximum) since 2002, and there had been only a limited number of incidents. However, British troops, who took the lead in

Helmand, have acted as a magnet for Taliban groups. Taliban propaganda has portrayed the southward expansion of NATO as a threat to opium cultivation, even though counter-narcotics is not part of NATO's mandate.[8] As of August 2007, the total number of British military casualties stood at 73 soldiers killed in action, most of them in Helmand province.

With the insurgency gaining momentum, the shift towards a war-fighting rather than a peacekeeping and stabilisation approach is unlikely to be reversed. Nonetheless, there are significant disagreements among NATO states over deployments. During the November 2006 NATO summit in Riga, the depth of these divisions was made abundantly clear. A handful of NATO countries – the US, Canada, the UK and the Netherlands – have borne much of the combat burden. These nations have urged other NATO states to remove or relax the restrictions they have placed on what their military forces can do in Afghanistan. Most NATO countries operating in Afghanistan have refused to allow their soldiers to engage in combat, and have ensured that they are deployed to stable parts of the country. France, Italy, Germany and Spain have agreed to remove their caveats in an emergency, to support embattled NATO troops, but have ruled out deploying combat forces to the south.[9]

'Ink Spots'

The 'Ink Spot' strategy was introduced by Lieutenant-General David Richards, then British ISAF commander in Afghanistan, in May 2006.[10] The goal of the strategy is to create areas of security and stability where development projects could be implemented. Over time, these islands of stability (dubbed Afghan Development Zones (ADZs)) could be linked together. According to Lieutenant-General Karl Eikenberry, former commander of Coalition forces in Afghanistan, the Ink Spots are intended 'to deny the enemy safe havens, to interdict his movement routes and, most importantly, to extend the authority of the central government'.[11]

Since their arrival in Helmand, British troops have been under constant fire in the 'platoon houses' established in the government district centres of Musa Qala, Sangin, Nowzad and Kajaki, and are unable to carry out the reconstruction tasks entailed in the Ink Spot strategy. In parallel with the deals reached with the Taliban leadership in Pakistan, a controversial arrangement was brokered in Musa Qala through the former (pro-British) governor, Mohammed Daud. The 'cessation of fighting'[12] agreement made with 'village elders' led to the withdrawal of British troops and Taliban fighters. Although the situation rapidly improved, by setting such a precedent NATO may have encouraged the creation of vacuums that the Taliban could fill. According to Haji Malang, the Musa Qala police chief: 'They [the Taliban] have their place which we cannot enter and we have our place and they must not come in'.[13] Musa Qala was later taken over by the Taliban. Nonetheless, the Ink Spot strategy meets a clear need for NATO and the Coalition, which, while it has won tactical victories against the Taliban, has been unable to hold or consolidate its gains.[14] ADZs are designed to do just that by fostering development and good governance in the wake of operations to clear out insurgents.

Provincial Reconstruction Teams (PRTs)

Provincial Reconstruction Teams have been key implementing actors of the Ink Spot strategy. Originally a US creation designed by the Department of Defense and the US Agency for International Development (USAID), and modelled on a similar concept to the CORDS programme (Civil Operations and Rural Development Support) in Vietnam, PRTs are joint civil–military teams typically comprising 80–250 personnel. They are intended to 'win hearts and minds' and to jumpstart the reconstruction effort in their areas of operation. The idea behind the PRTs is to break the vicious cycle of insecurity and obstructed development; as Eikenberry repeatedly emphasised: 'Where the road ends, the Taliban begins'.

When it was introduced, the PRT model raised concerns among NGOs that it would blur the distinction between the military and civilian aid agencies. The goals of humanitarian agencies and militaries differ: while the primary objective of NGOs is the provision of aid in response to humanitarian needs, this is only a secondary objective to the military, behind counter-insurgency. A military presence within the humanitarian space (defined as 'the access and freedom for humanitarian organizations to assess and meet humanitarian needs', according to the European Commission's Directorate for Humanitarian Aid) can indeed make NGOs uncomfortable by aligning them with military objectives. According to NATO, the PRTs have three primary objectives: 'to help the Government of Afghanistan extend its authority, to facilitate the development of a secure environment in the Afghan regions, including the establishment of relationships with local authorities, [and] to support, as appropriate, security-sector reform activities, within means and capabilities, to facilitate the reconstruction effort'.[15]

The first PRT was introduced in Gardez in January 2003. Since then, 25 have been deployed across the country. The expansion of these teams was planned in four stages, starting from Kabul. Stage 1 (North) involved a German-led PRT in Kunduz (which came under ISAF's authority on 30 December 2003). In June 2004, the transfer of the two UK-led PRTs in

Meymana to Norway and Mazar-i Sharif to Sweden with its Forward Support Base (a logistic hub), together with the establishment of another German-led PRT in Feyzabad and a Dutch-led PRT in Pol-i-Kumri, completed the first stage. Stage 2 (West) started in 2005, when the US PRT in Farah and the Italian one in Herat came under ISAF's control. In Stage 3 (South), the UK took over responsibility for the PRT in Lashkar Gah, the provincial capital of Helmand, in May 2006. On 5 October 2006, Stage 4 (West) saw NATO take command of the US and Coalition PRTs in eastern Afghanistan.

Although all the PRTs in Afghanistan are under NATO command, they each operate according to the rules and caveats of the nation running them, employing, according to Robert Perito, an 'ad hoc approach to security and development'.[16] Perito has underlined the lack of a coordinated approach and the emphasis on quick-impact projects and self-protection as some of the main problems with the PRT model. Another major limitation is the lack of training and preparation in development work provided to civilian and military PRT personnel. Tours are short, and there is no overarching institution to analyse and disseminate lessons learned. The fact that PRTs are not designed according to a uniform model could, however, be justified on the ground that each province and district poses different problems. As Lieutenant-General David Barno, a former commander of US and Coalition forces in Afghanistan, put it in May 2004: 'one size does not fit all'.[17] In reality, the lack of uniformity has more to do with Western governments' reluctance to deploy forces in potentially volatile parts of the country, where they would engage in combat operations. Hence another criticism of the concept: PRTs are too light to affect the socio-economical landscape, and too busy on non-combat tasks to ensure their own protection.

Several recommendations have been made to enhance the PRT model, starting with a US Institute of Peace report in September 2005.[18] The most notable are:

- Greater emphasis on security, particularly in the least-secure provinces, with aid provided only in emergency situations.
- The preservation of 'humanitarian space'; humanitarian agencies do not want to be perceived as part of a military campaign plan (and they want to remove conditionalities on assistance, such as intelligence collaboration).
- A shift from quick-impact projects towards infrastructure rehabilitation.
- Coordinate projects and share information with humanitarian agencies.

Paradoxically, the establishment of PRTs has been accompanied by rising insecurity, with the exception of Mazar-i Sharif. As the insurgency was regrouping and getting organised, PRTs were not primary targets. But following NATO's expansion and the roll-out of PRTs all over Afghanistan, an extended range of foreign military targets in the heartland of the insurgency became available as the Taliban grew stronger and focused on disrupting PRT operations and countering NATO's Ink Spot strategy. Because of the PRTs' mission, force-protection focus and small size, it is important to keep in mind that they are not the main tool for providing security in the country, but rather are there to help establish development and stability.

A test for military transformation

Western armies in Afghanistan have confronted unexpected challenges in the asymmetric attrition warfare they have faced. Most NATO forces have lacked adequate equipment and training to fight these operations, starting with inadequate information-operations officers and unreliable human intelligence on the ground. Certain technological elements, such as the increased use of UAVs, have compensated to some extent for these deficiencies. French *Sperwers*, German *Lunas* and US *Global Hawk* and *Predator* UAVs – the latter is the only one carrying firepower – have provided better battlespace awareness, though there has perhaps been an over-reliance on this technology.[19] At the other end of the warfare spectrum, special-operations officers working in Afghanistan have called for more flexible missions outside of large army manoeuvres, and have complained of cumbersome chains of command leading to delays between the identification of a target on the ground and the order to engage it.[20]

As Afghanistan confirmed its geostrategic importance at the turn of the century, the world's most formidable military alliance has pledged to be the guarantor of its security, unearthing unseen challenges which are proving to be the ultimate test for NATO's future. US and ISAF support in fighting the radical insurgency brings a long-term commitment that has to be not only sustained, but reinforced as time goes by. PRTs also represent an innovative way for NATO to fulfil its stabilisation objectives, provided that this initiative is strengthened. By adding a counter-insurgency role to a peacekeeping one, NATO and its partners have shown their sense of adaptation and their will to succeed, even at such a distance from their traditional theatre of operation. The US military too seems to have readjusted its focus on Afghanistan. The country's past three decades of war and internal conflict have reinforced radical Islamist elements, making them part of Afghanistan's socio-religious fabric. As far as the international military presence is concerned, and beyond its central role in security-sector reform, combating the threats to Afghanistan's security calls for the right mix of soft (as in the PRTs) and hard power – including a commitment from NATO and ISAF members to relax their national caveats in order to take on offensive actions when needed.

CHAPTER FIVE

Security-Sector Reform

This chapter analyses the process of reconstructing and transforming the security architecture of the Afghan state, known as security-sector reform (SSR). The steady deterioration in security in Afghanistan since 2001 has put SSR at the forefront of the state-building process. The 2001 Bonn Agreement addressed the security sector only superficially, with vague provisions for the extension of state authority over militias and the establishment of a Judicial Reform Commission. By 2003, however, Karzai was referring to the SSR process as the 'basic pre-requisite to [sic] recreating the nation that today's parents hope to leave to future generations'.[1] Despite the growing recognition of the importance of SSR, the meaning of the concept has gradually been obscured and distorted. SSR is not merely a modern euphemism for the training and equipping of security forces, the most common form of Western security assistance to developing states during the Cold War. Rather, it embraces a holistic vision of the security sector, one which balances the need to enhance the operational effectiveness of the security forces with the need to ensure that they are subordinated to democratic civilian authority and conform to international norms of human rights. This model of security assistance expands the boundaries of the security sector by recognising the symbiotic relationship between the security forces and the judicial system. In line with the growing awareness of the nexus between security and development in the wake of the Cold War, SSR seeks to advance the security of people, rather than regimes.

Although the SSR model was well developed and widely embraced in the international development and security communities by the time the Taliban fell in 2001, its influence over Afghanistan's SSR process has been short lived, and over time the process has regressed into a Cold War-era train-and-equip programme. This has stemmed largely from the failure of international military forces to provide an adequate security buffer for the state-building project, compelling the government and donors to see the SSR process, particularly as it concerns the nascent Afghan security forces, as the principal mechanism to address immediate security threats. The resultant focus on improving the operational effectiveness of the security forces has drawn attention and resources away from judicial reform and initiatives to establish an effective system of democratic oversight. Many of the problems that confront the SSR process today can be traced back to the 'slide toward expediency' in its implementation.[2]

One of the principal obstacles to the effective realisation of reform has been the framework established to support it.[3] At a Group of Eight (G8) donors' conference in Geneva in April 2002, the SSR agenda was formally set with the establishment of the lead-nation system. The security sector was divided into five pillars, and a lead nation was appointed to oversee reforms in each.[4] The five pillars were: military reform (the US); police reform (Germany); judicial reform (Italy); the disarmament, demobilisation and reintegration (DDR) of former combatants (Japan); and counter-narcotics (the UK). By tying individual donors to specific areas of the reform agenda, the system was intended to ensure the balanced distribution of resources and durable donor engagement. However, no mechanism was established to harmonise the activities of the lead nations or build synergies among them, undercutting one of the core precepts of the SSR model, namely the need for a holistic and integrated approach. Some donors assumed that the Afghan government would take on the role of tying together donor activities, but acute shortfalls in capacity prevented it from doing so. Whilst the system succeeded in firmly affixing the lead donors to their pillars, it also made them territorial. Donors were often more concerned with protecting their turf than advancing SSR more widely. Moreover, the system did not adequately consider differences between donors in competencies or resources. This contributed to significant imbalances and massive resource disparities between the pillars. As a result, the pace and achievements of reform have differed widely. By the start of 2007, it had become clear that, given the integrated nature of the security sector, such differentiation was damaging. Advances in deploying newly trained police, for instance, were being undermined by a lack of progress in the reform of the judicial system.

Military reform

The achievements of the military-reform pillar have far outpaced the rest of the SSR agenda, largely because it has been extremely well resourced relative to the other four pillars. By the end of 2005, approximately $3.5bn had been spent on reforms of the defence sector, compared to only $900m on the police.[5] Although military reform will invariably be the most resource-intensive component of any SSR agenda, this gap is nonetheless striking. The reform process has two components: the creation of the ANA and reform of the Defence Ministry.

The Afghan National Army (ANA)

At the Bonn II conference in December 2002, Karzai issued a decree formally establishing the Afghan National Army. The decree set a troop threshold of 70,000 and outlined the organisational structure of the army and of the Defence Ministry. Both the government and the international donor community saw the ANA as the key to restoring 'security, the rule-of-law and the full exercise of human rights throughout the country'.[6] The decree was the product of months of wrangling over the size of the ANA among the Defence Ministry, ISAF, the United States and other international actors. The US and ISAF advocated the creation of a small force of no more than 50,000, while a paper circulated by the Defence Ministry called for an army of 200,000.[7] The then Defence Minister, Mohammad Qasim Fahim, a leader of the mainly Tajik Shura-i Nezar faction of the Northern Alliance, sought to fill the ranks of the army with members of the Afghan Military Force (AMF), the assemblage of militias that had previously formed the Northern Alliance, and which had been recast to serve as the country's military arm until a new army could be constituted. The final plan for the force favoured the wholesale recreation of the ANA, accepted only minimal engagement by former mujahadeen fighters – the majority of whom were to be demobilised and reintegrated into civilian life through the Japanese-led DDR process – and eschewed the notion of a reserve force in favour of a highly mobile and professional army.

Training of the first class of ANA recruits began on 14 May 2002, at the country's former military academy on the outskirts of Kabul, renamed the Kabul Military Training Center (KMTC). A special Coalition Joint Task Force was set up, dubbed Task Force Phoenix, to oversee the training. The Defence Ministry stated in its October 2004 *National Military Strategy* that the end-state of the process was an ANA that would 'strongly and seriously avoid political, factional, group, ethnic and other discriminatory tendencies … conforming to modern standards and principles practiced in coalition and democratic countries'.[8] While the US maintains overall control of the training programme, France assumed responsibility for training the officer corps, and the UK for training non-commissioned officers (NCOs). By November 2006, 14 different countries had joined Task Force Phoenix, which consisted of 4,695 personnel (2,748 of whom were American). The task force operated under the umbrella of the US Office of Military Cooperation–Afghanistan (OMC-A),[9] the body established to oversee the overall development of the ANA, including its force structure, chain of command, logistics, physical infrastructure and equipment procurement.

The training programme was originally based on a ten-week cycle, with two *kandaks* (battalions), numbering 500–600 troops, trained simultaneously. In an effort to accelerate the process and to compensate for a growing desertion rate, the US increased the number of *kandaks* trained simultaneously to five in November 2004.[10] It was hoped that this adjustment would allow the programme to complete all training by September 2007. The training schedule was also increased to 12 weeks – including basic training, advanced individual training and collective training – to improve the quality of the troops produced. However, the training process focused disproportionately on combat troops and overlooked sustaining commands. Although approximately 20,000 combat troops had been trained by 2005, only 1,300 of the 21,000 positions in the sustaining commands had been filled.[11] This made it very difficult for the force to operate independently without Coalition logistical support. As one Combined Security Transition Command–Afghanistan (CSTC-A) official remarked in June 2006: 'The main goal of the process was to get the ANA into the fight'.[12] In an apparent effort to resolve, or at least circumvent, this problem, the OMC-A adjusted the force structure, reducing the number of personnel authorised for the sustaining commands to 14,000 in May 2005. According to Eikenberry, the issue was not that the sustaining commands were being overlooked, but that their training and development took longer.[13] The revised US plan envisioned four sustaining commands – Recruiting, Education and Training, Acquisitions and Logistics and Communications and Intelligence – being fully operational by the end of 2007.[14] The problems encountered in staffing the sustaining commands, coupled with growing awareness that the government was incapable of meeting the recurrent budgetary expenditures of the rapidly expanding force, prompted the US to slow down the training process in early 2006, reducing the number of *kandaks* trained concurrently to three or four.[15] As of April 2007 there were 8,700 recruits undergoing basic training at the KMTC.[16]

Under the Afghanistan Compact, the successor to the Bonn Agreement signed at a conference in London in January–February 2006, a new deadline was set for the ANA development process. The Compact asserts that, by the end of 2010, 'a nationally respected, professional, ethnically balanced Afghan National Army will be fully established that is democratically accountable, organized, trained and equipped to meet the security needs of the country and increasingly funded from Government revenue, commensurate with the nation's economic capacity'.[17] However, like many other plans and timelines set for the ANA since its formation in 2002, this was quickly superseded. In November 2006, Defence Minister Rahim Wardak asserted during a trip to the United States that the new goal was to complete the training of all 70,000 ANA troops by October 2008.[18] The revised plan was contingent on an increase in US funding. In January 2007 Bush announced that the administration would ask Congress for $10.6bn in supplemental aid for Afghanistan, $8.6bn of which would be allocated to the security forces.[19]

The issue of the ANA's size, hotly debated in 2002, was reopened in early 2006, when then US Defense Secretary Donald Rumsfeld reportedly informed the Afghan government that the ceiling for the force would be reduced to 45,000 soldiers, a decision made unilaterally without Afghan consultation.[20] The US was responding to a World Bank report released in late 2005 which outlined acute problems in the fiscal sustainability of the security sector. According to the report, in the 2004/05 financial year the ANA had cost the equivalent of 293% of domestic revenue and 13% of GDP.[21] With the government assuming responsibility for paying ANA salaries in 2006, and with recurrent costs steadily increasing, the fiscal burden of a 70,000-troop force was deemed too great.[22] US officials accompanied the decision with assurances that Afghanistan would come under the security umbrella of the US, safeguarding it from external threats. Nonetheless, many actors in the Afghan government, particularly in the Defence Ministry, revived calls for an expansion of the force. In July 2006, Wardak claimed that the government could not secure the country with an army smaller than 150,000 troops.[23] Wardak made his case for a larger ANA on the basis of cost efficiency. According to his calculations, the cost of deploying one Coalition soldier could fund 50–100 Afghan troops.[24] Other members of the government have called for the re-introduction of a conscript army – the norm prior to the civil war, and a less costly system that could generate the necessary increases in manpower.[25] However, moving from a volunteer, professional army to a conscript force would be a dramatic change in course, and is unlikely to be endorsed by the US. In any case, the threats posed by the insurgency demand highly specialised and agile forces, not massive troop formations. The deadlock was apparently resolved with Bush's request for increased funding for the security forces in early 2007. Nonetheless, the episode demonstrated continuing tensions within the military-reform process, and its tenuous ownership by the government.

ANA units have reportedly performed well in the field, with up to 12 *kandaks* operationally deployed across the country in the spring of 2005.[26] They operated in conjunction with NATO and Coalition forces in every major military operation of 2006, including *Mountain Lion, Mountain Thrust* and *Medusa*.[27] In August 2006, the ANA conducted its first battalion-sized combat operation, which combined logistics, mortars, scouts and infantry from several different companies.[28] Although closely monitored and supported by Coalition Embedded Training Teams (ETTs), the mission was nonetheless viewed as a milestone in the development of the ANA, which has found it difficult to end its dependence on international military forces.

The ETTs, which comprised over 800 mentors in June 2006, have been instrumental in the development of the ANA. They operate at corps, brigade, battalion and company levels, ranging in size from eight to 16 personnel.[29] In addition, as NATO has expanded its military presence across the country, it has gradually assumed a more prominent role in the development of the Afghan security forces, and has begun to deploy its own units, dubbed Operational Mentoring and Liaison Teams (OMLTs).[30] The OMLTs typically consist of 12–19 personnel, and deploy for six-month periods.[31] The role of the ETTs and OMLTs is multifaceted and extends beyond the provision of training to soldiers, officers and NCOs, to include assisting in the development of basic systems, such as personnel and logistics, and accompanying units into combat.[32]

Given the high rates of illiteracy in Afghanistan and the paucity of professional military experience, developing leadership has been one of the principal problems in setting up the ANA. To address this, the CSTC-A has overseen the establishment of a National Military Academy of Afghanistan (NMAA) and a Command and General Staff College. On 22 March 2005, the NMAA began training its first class of 109 cadets. Modelled on the US military academy at West Point, the NMAA is a four-year, degree-granting institution.[33] While the Afghan government experienced difficulties in recruiting qualified candidates for the first class of the NMAA, this has not posed a problem since. Over 1,400 applicants, the bulk of whom met the basic educational criteria for entry, applied for the 350 places available for the third class of the academy, which will graduate in 2011.[34] The Command and General Staff College, modelled after the US Army and NATO equivalent, opened its doors to its first class of army and police officers on 28 October 2006.[35] It prepares officers to take on command assignments from the battalion level upwards.[36] The US has also prioritised building up the NCO corps, seen as the backbone of modern volunteer armies. In addition to the specialised NCO training provided at the KMTC, Mobile Training Teams (MTTs) offer targeted training.[37] As of June 2006, four MTTs were in operation, each comprising three trainers.[38]

By April 2007, approximately 35,000 ANA troops had been trained and deployed, taking the force halfway to its goal of 70,000 personnel.[39] However, these impressive figures, and the modest battlefield achievements of the ANA, should not distract attention away from the significant problems the force continues to face. Paramount among these is the issue of troop retention. In mid 2003, the attrition rate for the army reached a high of 10% per month.[40] A number of factors explain why Afghans were leaving the force in such high numbers. Firstly, pay was incommensurate with the cost of living. The initial salary for a rank-and-file ANA soldier was $50 per month; this was raised to $70 in 2004, and to $100 in late 2006.[41] Although the current salary is double the average wage for an Afghan civil servant, it is below the $150 which US planners determined in 2003 would be needed to keep soldiers in the ranks.[42] In the light of the Afghan government's limited revenue-generating capacity, it is unlikely that salaries will be raised further in the foreseeable future. Compounding the problem of salaries is the lack of an effective mechanism for soldiers on deployment to deliver their salaries to their families; soldiers regularly take unauthorised leave from their units to do this. While the US has instituted a number of stop-gap measures to deal with the problem in the short term, such as providing leave to soldiers immediately after the delivery of salary payments, a permanent solution has not been found. The US military has spent two years developing a computerised salary-payment system, but this has yet to become fully operational.[43]

Secondly, there was palpable discontent early on in the process with living conditions, food and the lack of adequate mosques on military bases. The US has since addressed these issues through intensive projects to build and refurbish military facilities. In September 2004, the US Defense Security Cooperation Agency awarded a $1bn contract to the Army Corps of Engineers to build vital ANA infrastructure, including a central command in Kabul and four regional commands.

Thirdly, the lack of ethnic balance in the force in the year after it was created encouraged desertions. The ANA included a disproportionately large number of Tajiks, and a small number of Pashtuns. According to some estimates, the army was up to 40% Tajik in 2002, more than double the Tajik share of the wider population, while 37% was Pashtun, well below their share nationally. The remaining ethnic groups – the Hazara, Uzbeks and Turkomen – fared even worse. This ethnic imbalance can largely be attributed to Tajik dominance of the Defence Ministry, where Fahim used his position to pack the ranks with Shura-i Nezar loyalists. For instance, of the 38 generals Fahim appointed to the reconstituted General Staff in February 2002, 37 were Tajiks.[44] Ninety of the first 100 generals appointed by Fahim were affiliated with Shura-i Nezar.[45] This ethnic imbalance aroused fears among the Pashtun and northern minority communities that the army was merely an extension of the Shura-i Nezar faction, making recruitment from these groups difficult and preventing the formation of a national ethos or *esprit de corps* in the military. To address this problem the US instituted an ethnic-quota system in 2003. As the most recent census in Afghanistan was undertaken in 1979, the baseline figures were taken from the *CIA Factbook*.[46] By 2006, the ethnic composition of the army had been brought within the designated tolerance levels.[47] By 2006, the Coalition tended to see the problem of ethnic balance as resolved, but minority groups, notably the Hazara, continued to complain about under-representation.[48]

Finally, the intensity of counter-insurgency operations in the south, coupled with displeasure over long deployments away from home regions and families, provided a major incentive for soldiers to desert. In 2003 and 2004, desertions spiked following engagements with the resurgent Taliban in the south.

Steps taken to counter desertions succeeded in lowering the attrition rate to 1–2% per month by late 2006 – still a worrying figure, but one within the expectations of US planners. At the same time, however, the number of soldiers going absent without leave (AWOL) reached alarming levels. According to a representative of the US private security company Military Professional Resources Incorporated (MPRI), 40% of a typical battalion is AWOL at any one time.[49] A Personnel Asset Inventory conducted by the Coalition at the Herat Regional Corps of the ANA in 2006 was able to account for only 4,000 of the corps' 10,000 personnel.[50] Meanwhile, the US estimates that as many as 20% of ANA troops are likely not to re-enlist once their standard three-year service contract has expired.[51] Some sources in the Western donor community claim that the problem is much more severe even than this, asserting that the re-enlistment rate is as low as 20–35%.[52] Colonel Abdul Raziq, a brigade commander in southern Afghanistan, stated in November 2006 that 'for every 1,000 recruits who graduate from basic training, at least 500 will leave after three years to find other work – either in Afghanistan or Pakistan or Iran'.[53] Raziq, like many others, attributes the widespread failure to re-enlist to the inadequacy of the monthly salary, an issue that the increase to $100 per month was intended to resolve.

Against this, recruiting numbers have been robust. Difficulties attracting qualified recruits early in the process were addressed through the establishment of the ANA Recruiting Command (ANAREC) and 35 National Army Volunteer Centers, one in each province. Staffed by 176 trained recruitment officers, the centres surpassed their target of 10,450 recruits in 2006, and were expected to meet their target of 14,000 in 2007.[54] The ANAREC applies a set of enlistment criteria intended to ensure the highest standard of recruits entering the force, and to reduce factional infiltration. The upper age limit of 28 set for recruits disqualifies the majority of jihadi fighters and factional militiamen. Additional vetting procedures include provisions that all candidates meet certain physical standards, have no criminal background and are not affiliated to any armed groups.[55] The latter two conditions, the lynchpin of the vetting system, depend on reliable information such as criminal records. The lack of such information, coupled with intense pressure to accelerate recruitment to meet force targets, means that the ANA has been infiltrated by factional militias and even Taliban sympathisers.[56] In an effort to address this problem, which is present in the police as well as the ANA, the government and the Coalition have introduced a 'vouching system', whereby an individual wishing to join the military must be vouched for by a tribal or village elder, who attests to their integrity and commitment to the government.[57] Recruits are then required to sign an oath of loyalty to the government. While Major-General Robert Durbin, the commander of the CSTC-A in the summer of 2006, has described this as 'one of the key aspects of ensuring the quality and integrity of the members of the police force and the army', the system is vulnerable to manipulation, most obviously in cases where community leaders themselves sympathise with the Taliban or other spoiler groups.[58]

In addition to issues of personnel strength and quality, shortfalls in equipment have seriously degraded the ANA's operational capacity. One of the Defence Ministry's biggest complaints concerns weapons. First Deputy Minister Yusuf Nuristani affirmed in 2006 that 'every soldier has a weapon, but some don't work after five shots'.[59] ANA weapons have come from three sources: donated equipment, primarily from former Eastern bloc countries; weapons collected under the auspices of the DDR programme; and transfers from the US. The initial US strategy was to rely heavily on donations from former Eastern bloc countries, on the basis that Afghans were most familiar with Soviet weapons, notably the *Kalashnikov* assault rifle. However, a large proportion of the equipment donated by foreign states was 'worn out, defective, or incompatible with existing equipment'.[60] Meanwhile, weapons transfers from the DDR programme were well below expectations, and much of what was transferred was barely serviceable. In response to these problems, and growing Afghan exhortations for US-made weaponry, notably M-16 rifles, the US changed its equipment strategy. In 2006, it announced the donation of $2bn worth of US-made military equipment to the ANA, reportedly including 2,500 'Humvees', tens of thousands of M-16s and 20,000 sets of bullet-proof helmets and flak jackets.[61] More equipment is expected to be purchased from the $8.6bn allocated for the security forces under Bush's 2007 supplemental budget request. These funds are likely to be spent on communications and airlift. Some ANA commanders are forced to use mobile phones in the absence of a secure communications system, and the ANA continues to rely on Coalition aircraft to transport its troops around the country.[62]

Reform of the Defence Ministry

Reforms of the Defence Ministry were under-resourced and largely over-looked until the latter half of 2004. Following his victory in the October 2004 presidential elections, Karzai replaced Defence Minister Fahim with Wardak, a Western-oriented professional soldier. Fahim had been one of the principal obstacles to reform during his tenure as defence minister, and US investment was minimal when set against the problems the Defence Ministry faced. Some reforms were implemented, largely consisting of mentoring senior ministry officials and establishing some core systems, tasks that were contracted to MPRI. At an early stage in the process, however, it became clear that reform efforts would be fruitless without a change in leadership and the 'defactionalisation' of the ministry.

Japanese pressure elicited the first major personnel reforms. The Japanese government made its funds for the Afghan New Beginnings Programme (ANBP), the DDR initiative, conditional on the implementation of personnel changes in the Defence Ministry to instil in it greater professionalism and ethnic balance. Twenty-two new appointments were made in September 2003, affecting all the senior positions in the ministry, including five deputy ministers. The following December, 104 new mid-level appointments were made, followed by another 330 in April–May

2004.[63] The erosion of Fahim's power under the weight of international and intra-governmental pressure paved the way for his removal from the cabinet in October 2004.

In many respects, Wardak's appointment can be considered the beginning of the US-led reform process within the Defence Ministry. The existing MPRI programme was significantly expanded and accelerated. By June 2006, 23 MPRI mentors were advising senior officials. All told, 50 MPRI staff were working in the ministry, overseeing the creation of 22 major systems, ranging from strategic planning to personnel management.[64] Most of these systems, which are based on US and NATO models, had to be set up from scratch.[65] Although MPRI advisers are directing all aspects of the reform process, from writing policy to setting administrative structures, they liaise closely with their Afghan counterparts through working groups established around key issue areas.[66] MPRI also provides capacity development in the form of training courses for new and existing staff, lasting for two to four days.[67] While training is vital to build capacity in the ministry, much of what has been provided has focused on high-level policy issues; according to one international adviser, officials 'still don't know the nuts and bolts' of ministry business, such as how to run a meeting.[68] While reforms between 2004 and 2006 certainly improved the professionalism and efficiency of a ministry that, under Fahim, was one of the most corrupt and factionalised in the government, one Western adviser warned in late 2005 that 'the pace of reform and the desire to deliver is faster than the Afghan Ministry of Defence, and for that matter any Western military, can handle'.[69] Although the Defence Ministry demonstrated increased independence and assertiveness during 2006, it remains heavily dependent on the Coalition to set policy and manage and support the fledgling ANA.

Police reform

At 8am on 29 May 2006, a large cargo truck at the head of a US military convoy experienced a 'mechanical failure' that caused it to smash into 12 cars stopped in rush-hour traffic near Kabul.[70] The incident, in which five civilians were killed, prompted rioting across Kabul, resulting in at least 17 more deaths; 190 people were injured, and the damage ran into millions of dollars.[71] Hundreds of men and boys, many brandishing assault rifles, attacked the offices of international organisations, guesthouses, restaurants and government buildings. The police failed to stop the rioters from reaching the administrative centre of Kabul. Many fled checkpoints as the mobs approached, and some officers took off their uniforms and joined the rioters. According to Paul Barker, the country director of the international humanitarian NGO CARE International, the police were involved in the looting and torching of CARE's Kabul office.[72] A representative of another international NGO ransacked during the riots claimed that the police demanded payments to protect their premises.[73] When police officers did stand their ground, they proved inadequately trained and equipped to confront the situation. Most had received no training in crowd control and lacked non-lethal equipment like riot gear, water hoses and tear gas.[74] Instead, they used guns to disperse the crowds, in many cases inflaming the situation.

The rioting highlighted the ineptitude of the police and the failure of four years of police reform, which from its outset has been under-resourced, poorly planned and plagued by problems of coordination and capacity deficits. Since 2002, the Afghan National Police (ANP) has been a source of insecurity for communities across the country, rather than a solution to it. A significant proportion of Afghans view the police with fear and resentment. When they interact with the police, it is often to pay bribes or illegal taxes. Corruption, much of it linked to the drug trade, is endemic.[75] The amount of money earned through corruption ranges from $200 per month for a patrolman to $30,000 per month for a police general.[76] Police officers perpetrate crimes ranging from kidnapping for ransom to bank robberies, fuelling a rising countrywide crime rate.[77] The offences most commonly reported as being committed by police in 2004 were failure to prosecute murder cases and torture.[78] In November 2004, an AIHRC spokesperson claimed that 15% of all human-rights violations reported over the previous six months had been carried out by the police. In addition, a majority of the police are loyal to regional commanders rather than the Interior Ministry, a by-product of the heavy factionalisation of the force.

The police-reform process was formally launched in March 2002, with the signature of an agreement between the Afghan Interior Ministry and its German counterpart. The German Police Project Office (GPPO) opened on 3 April 2002. The GPPO, whose staff has ranged from 25 to 39, is tasked with training the police, supporting the re-establishment of a police academy, implementing bilateral police funding assistance and coordinating international support for the reform process.[79]

Germany has adopted a distinctly different approach to police reform than that pursued by the United States in developing the ANA. Whereas the ANA was a new entity constructed from the ground up, the Germans sought to transform existing police structures and personnel. This approach was dictated primarily by resource constraints, as the German government was not prepared to allocate the funds that would have been needed to recreate the force from scratch. Moreover, disbanding the police was not seen as a viable option due to the security vacuum this would create, and the resentment it would arouse among existing officers.

At the outset of the process, the Afghan government endorsed a force ceiling for a police force of 62,000, based on calculations by German and Afghan planners.[80] According to one former senior Interior Ministry official, this figure was roughly derived from the ratio of police to citizens applied in Germany (1:500). However, this formula was not applicable in a country facing a legacy of war, with rugged topography and low population density.[81] In 2007 the force target was increased to 82,000, including 18,500 border police, in response to rising insecurity. However, even at this new force ceiling Afghanistan will have the smallest per capita police force in the region. A suitable comparison is Iraq, whose population of 27m is comparable to that of Afghanistan. Its police force stood at 152,000 in May 2006, with plans to expand it to 190,000.[82]

Between 2002 and 2006, the GPPO administered $80m in German assistance.[83] The flagship initiative was the rehabilitation of the National Police Academy, which offers training for commissioned officers, known as *Saran*, and non-commissioned personnel, referred to as *Satanman*, through three-year and one-year courses respectively. Although the GPPO developed the curriculum for the academy, a Norwegian Police Project has designed and implemented specialised training modules in human rights, management and gender issues.[84] By the beginning of 2006, 3,302 individuals had graduated from the academy, comprising 251 *Saran*, 2,299 *Satanman* and 752 border police.[85] While the German programme effectively established a system to reconstitute the middle and higher ranks of the police, it largely overlooked the ordinary ranks, the patrolmen or *Satunkai*, who represented the main interface with the population. The bulk of the police in the country were former militiamen who lacked any semblance of formal training, and whose 'militiamen's mentality' was not conducive to effective community policing.[86]

The slow progress of police reforms had a cascading effect throughout the entire security sector, prompting the US to enter the process in early 2003. In 2003 and 2004, US support focused on establishing a constabulary training system for Afghanistan's ordinary police. The US-based company DynCorp International was contracted to construct a Central Training Center (CTC) in Kabul and seven Regional Training Centers (RTCs), in Kandahar, Gardez, Jalalabad, Bamiyan, Kunduz, Mazar-i Sharif and Herat, and to implement a training curriculum developed by the US Department of Justice's International Investigative Training Assistance Program.[87] The US programme greatly accelerated the pace of training; by the end of 2004, over 32,000 police officers had been trained, and by July 2007 that number had swelled to 71,147.[88] However, the quality of the training is questionable. The programme offers three core courses: a five-week course for illiterate officers; a nine-week course for literate officers; and a 15-day Transition Integration Program (TIP), which provides training for 'veteran police'.[89] Considering that more than 70% of ANP recruits are illiterate, only a small proportion of officers graduate from the nine-week programme, which comes closest to meeting basic standards of Western police education. According to US Department of Justice statistics, as of June 2006 only 10% of graduates had completed the nine-week programme. More than 40% had only completed the 15-day TIP programme. The US, Germany and Afghanistan have long talked about phasing out the programme for illiterate recruits, as so many basic police tasks depend on literacy. As a pilot project at the CTC, the US has launched a third basic course, which adds four weeks of literacy training to the existing nine-week course for literate officers; however, this has proven to be insufficient to bring recruits up to a basic level of literacy.

In June 2006, the Combined Security Transition Command Afghanistan (CSTC-A), which assumed overall responsibility for the provision of support to the police from the US Embassy's International Narcotics and Law Enforcement (INL) office in April 2005, reported that only 30,395 police officers met basic readiness criteria (the three criteria used were training received, unit staffing levels and equipment status).[90] In fact, on a four-point capability scale developed by the CSTC-A to measure the ANP's progress, the force was assessed at the lowest possible level, Capabilities Milestone 4. The goal is for the force to reach Capabilities Milestone 1, entailing a 'fully capable' and 'self-sustaining' force, by 2010.[91] Problems with force retention have cast serious doubt on whether this is achievable. Although there are no precise figures for the ANP's attrition rate, it is estimated at 15–30%.[92] This excessive figure can be attributed to a number of factors, including high casualty rates;[93] dissatisfaction over rates of pay; corruption; and family pressures.[94] As of July 2007, only 40% of the ANP were assessed to be adequately equipped.[95] The bulk of ANP equipment, notably small arms, have come from donations.[96] For instance, the Interior Ministry has received donations of weapons from Austria and Hungary, and vehicles from Russia, Germany and Japan. The wide range of countries making donations means that most of the equipment is non-standard, increasing maintenance and repair costs.[97]

A number of factors account for the poor readiness and performance of the police. Firstly, the ANP has found it difficult to find suitable recruits. Until 2006, ANP recruitment was ad hoc. Although the Training Department at the Interior Ministry is mandated to develop and oversee the application of general recruiting criteria and standards, in practice the National Police Academy, the CTC and the RTCs each apply their own criteria. Only the academy systematically screens entrants on the basis of the Interior Ministry's basic criteria of age, height, health and literacy.[98] The CTC and RTCs tend to test only for literacy in order to stream students into the appropriate training course. In 2006, steps were taken to strengthen the recruitment system. A recruiting headquarters was opened in July 2006, staffed by 85 newly trained recruiters. The ANP recruiters have been teamed with their ANA counterparts, who serve in a mentoring capacity. The plan is to assign one ANP recruiter to each province, with 3–5-strong recruitment teams based at each RTC.[99] Despite improvements to the recruiting system, vetting continues to pose a problem. Like the ANA, the ANP relies on a vouching system in which two individuals – who must be police officers, government officials or community leaders – endorse the candidacy of the individual for entry into the police. Voucher forms are subsequently reviewed by the Interior Ministry. However, many RTCs apply their own vetting procedures, and the high level of corruption at the ministry has meant that vetting procedures are routinely compromised. Moreover, without a reliable criminal-record database, it is impossible to prevent former criminals from entering the force.[100]

Related to the issue of vetting and recruitment is the endemic problem of factionalisation and ethnicity in the police. After the fall of the Taliban in 2001, the police became a dumping ground for AMF militiamen.[101] To circumvent the DDR process and protect their patronage networks, AMF commanders with positions in the police or civilian administration moved their militiamen into police units under their authority.[102] This trend was particularly apparent in the highway police, which was subsequently disbanded in 2006.[103] As one senior police official stated in June 2006: 'the ANP is not really a national police; police are loyal to local commanders'.[104] According to this official, he trusted fewer than 30 of the approximately 1,500 police stationed in Helmand.[105]

The lack of comprehensive in-service training or mentoring has compounded these problems. Police mentors were not deployed in Afghanistan until 2005, and even by the beginning of 2007 the number in the country was insufficient. By early 2007, the US had deployed approximately 500 mentors in the country, the bulk under contract through DynCorp.[106]

However, the restive south has been prioritised at the expense of the northern provinces.[107] Considering that over 800 mentors have been deployed to support the ANA, a significant increase in ANP mentors will be required to ensure appropriate geographical coverage. In February 2007, the European Union (EU) announced that it would deploy 160 police advisers, mentors and trainers, a move long urged by both Germany and the United States.[108] By June 2007, the European Policing Mission to Afghanistan (EUPOL) was operational and had brought the bulk of the non-US policing personnel in Afghanistan under its umbrella, including non-European actors. Aside from quantity, concerns have been raised about the quality of the trainers and mentors contracted by DynCorp. Then Interior Minister Jalali rejected 100 of the 150 trainers proposed by DynCorp for the police training programme in 2004.[109] According to a representative of the GPPO, some of the US mentors hired by DynCorp did not even have formal police training; some were private security guards or prison officers.[110]

Endemic corruption poses a further challenge to the reform process. The main driver of corruption in the police is the lucrative drug trade. Up to 80% of the police force are allegedly involved.[111] It has become conventional wisdom that one of the main causes of corruption is insufficient salaries. Until late 2005, the basic salary for an ANP patrolman was $30 per month, well below the average for the civil service.[112] In November 2005, the government approved a *tashkil*[113] for the ANP that increased the salary for an ANP patrolman to $70 per month, on a par with an ANA soldier. This salary increase came into effect in July 2006, but, while it may help to mitigate petty corruption, such as the levying of illegal road tolls, it will not be enough to compensate for the massive profits that can be accrued from involvement in the narcotics trade. Police chief positions in major drug-producing areas or in trafficking corridors are sold for anywhere between $20,000 and $100,000.[114] The lack of a computerised banking and salary-payment system early in the reform process meant that wages were often not effectively delivered to officers in the field. As late as June 2006, there were reports that some police officers had not received salaries for up to three months.[115] However, significant progress has been made to establish systems to more efficiently deliver salaries. Under the auspices of the CSTC-A, an Individual Payment System (IPS), in which Ministry of Finance personnel travel to the provinces to verify payroll lists and pay police, and an Electronic Funds Transfer (EFT) system, which transfers funds to individual bank accounts, were well advanced in their development by the end of 2006. The IPS was in operation in all but three provinces (Daikundi, Nimroz and Nuristan), while the EFT was being piloted in

Kabul and had resulted in the establishment of over 14,000 bank accounts for police officers. The goal is for all salary payments to be made through the EFT, but the lack of a countrywide banking system will probably delay this for several years.[116]

The principal source of funds to pay police salaries has been the Law and Order Trust Fund for Afghanistan (LOTFA), which was established under the auspices of UNDP in May 2002 to finance priority police activities, notably remuneration (salaries, allowances and other benefits). The fund was also designed to support the procurement of non-lethal equipment, the rehabilitation of police facilities and the strengthening of law-enforcement capacity across the country. The history of the LOTFA demonstrates one of the principal long-term problems facing the entire security sector, including the police: fiscal sustainability. LOTFA was created precisely because the government lacked the resources to finance a reformed ANP. Between 2002 and 2006, over $330m was channelled through the fund, the vast majority allocated to salaries. Currently in its fourth phase (April 2006–March 2008), the fund has found it very difficult to attract financing from donors.[117] While numerous donors, including Finland, Ireland, the UK and the Netherlands, contribute to the fund, it is dependent on donations from the European Community (EC) and the United States, which accounted for over 75% of all contributed funds by late 2006.[118] With the implementation of the new pay structure, the World Bank has estimated that salary costs for the police could increase to $177m a year, accounting for roughly a third of domestic revenue according to FY2005/06 figures.[119] Even an above-expected increase in state revenue over the coming decade will not offset this increase, meaning that international donors will have to support the Interior Ministry for the foreseeable future.

It is clear that intensive donor engagement in the police-reform process will be needed for up to a decade. If this engagement is to succeed, however, coordination among donors will have to improve. The reform process has never been conducted according to a clear strategic plan. Although the GPPO developed a reform strategy in 2003, this was not widely disseminated.[120] Until 2006, DynCorp refused to show its curriculum for the RTCs and CTC to the GPPO.[121] This typifies the tensions that have hindered cooperation between the two main donors to the police-reform process. These tensions have stemmed from two sources. The first is the differing policing and legal traditions of Germany and the United States, which have fostered different approaches to reform. The GPPO's approach is a product of the centralised German police tradition and the country's civil-code legal system. The US, by contrast, has a decentralised policing system and a legal code rooted in common law. Accordingly, the GPPO has advocated highly centralised police structures, while the US programme has emphasised community-policing models.[122] The second source of tension has been the G8 lead-nation system. US funding to the police between 2002 and 2006 was \$2.1bn. In May 2007, the US government committed an additional \$2.5bn to be spent by September 2008.[123] By contrast, Germany contributed a total of \$80m from 2002 to 2006. The massive disparity in spending between the two donors, incommensurate with Germany's lead-nation status, contributed to tensions between them. These were allayed somewhat following the 2006 London conference, which marked the end of the lead-nation system by formally passing lead responsibility to the Afghan government. Although Germany would maintain 'key partner' status, it would relinquish this to the EUPOL mission upon its inauguration in June 2007.[124]

Coordination between the German and US police missions improved markedly in late 2006 and early 2007. This improvement followed a meeting of police advisers in Dubai in April 2006, during which both missions resolved to work more closely together.[125] In the months following the meeting the CSTC-A accepted two advisers from the German police project. The pair serve as deputies to the heads of the two branches of the US policing mission, Task Force Police and the Police Reform Directorate (PRD). Task Force Police is mandated to oversee the training, mentoring and organisation of ANP units in the field, while the PRD is responsible for mentoring and training senior ANP staff, and implementing reforms at the central level.[126] Another important development indicative of a more cooperative approach between the two donors was the initiation of steps to coordinate the lesson plans of the National Police Academy and the US-sponsored training centres.[127]

A significant initiative to improve coordination and build synergies among all the stakeholders in the police-reform process took place in October 2006 with the introduction of the International Police Coordination Board (IPCB) at a second meeting of police advisors in Dubai.[128] The body, which features a standing secretariat, is intended to serve as the chief coordination forum at the strategic and operational levels. The first meeting of the IPCB, whose members include the Ministry of Interior, Germany, EUPOL, CSTC-A, ISAF, the UN Assistance Mission in Afghanistan (UNAMA), Norway, Canada, the UK and PRT and military liaison officers, took place in March 2007. Although the IPCB could play a vital role in bringing greater coordination and strategic direction to the reform process, its impact has been limited. Debates continue on whether it is a decision-making body or simply a forum for information sharing and dialogue.[129]

Perhaps the most important step in transforming the ANP came in 2006, with the launch of the Pay and Rank Reform process. The process is designed to implement the force structure embodied in the *tashkil* endorsed by the government in November 2005. Prior to the launch of the rank-reform component, the Interior Ministry and the police were extremely top-heavy, with field-grade and general officers outnumbering sergeants by three to two.[130] Rationalising the rank structure was intended to clarify and streamline the chain of command, ensuring that only qualified officials occupy the senior positions in the force. Implementing the *tashkil* will balance the system, reducing, for instance, the number of colonels from 2,447 to 235, while increasing the number of patrolmen from 36,600 to 45,880.[131] The process was intended to purge the police of unqualified and corrupt officials. It is a phased process, beginning with the most senior posts and working down to the rank of lieutenant.

The first stage, formally completed in early 2006, involved the appointment of 31 senior generals (two or three stars). The appointees were chosen via a three-stage selection process. After submitting an application, candidates were subjected to a file-review process, during which their education, professional experience, personal history and character were assessed. The next stage featured a written examination to assess the 'candidate's knowledge of the law and legal procedures, analytical abilities, management style and ethics'.[132] In the final stage, candidates were interviewed by a selection board consisting of the interior minister, two other senior members of the ministry and a representative from the German and US police missions. Each candidate who successfully completed the three stages was assigned a score, which was used to allocate a ranking. The ranked list was subsequently reviewed by the interior minister, and passed to the president for approval.

While the first phase of the process was seen as an unqualified success, the results of the second, focusing on one-star brigadier-generals, was mired in controversy. Among the positions affected were all 34 provincial police-chief posts. The controversy began with Karzai's decision to adjust the ranked list of 86 candidates submitted for final approval. Of the 50 amendments Karzai made to the list, the most noteworthy were his addition of 14 candidates who had not passed through the selection process.[133] Many, including the newly appointed police chief of Kabul, Amanullah Guzar, had dubious human-rights records. Karzai justified the additions on the basis of the need to ensure ethnic balance, as the original list featured only one Uzbek and very few Hazaras.[134] This did not mollify the GPPO, which argued that the manipulation of the list had tainted the process. Although the US also protested against the decision, it took a more prag-matic approach, arguing that results were more important than process and that 72 of the appointments were major improvements over their prede-cessors.[135] In response to the protestations of the international community, Karzai appointed a probation board to monitor the performance of the 14 disputed candidates and 'ensure that any confirmed appointments are made on the basis of merit, professionalism and integrity of the prospec-tive officials'.[136] The board consisted of six senior police generals, with Germany, the US, the EU and UNAMA attending as observers.[137] In January 2007, the probation board announced that it had rejected 11 of the 14 appointments under review.[138] In September 2006, Karzai signed a decree setting up a body intended to mitigate such problems in the future. The Special Consultative Board for Senior Level Appointments is mandated to approve senior-level appointments, including provincial police chiefs, in a transparent and accountable fashion. However, few appointments had been taken to the body for approval by mid 2007, and the government had not demonstrated much interest or faith in the board.[139]

The third and fourth phases of the process, which had yet to be completed in mid 2007, could be considered the most important as they will overhaul the intermediate ranks of the force. Phase 3, initially sched-uled for completion in early 2007, will address colonels and majors, filling 1,000 positions from a pool of 8,000 eligible applicants, while phase 4 will affect captains and lieutenants, appointing 5,000 company-grade offi-cers from a field of over 10,000.[140] The new pay scale is implemented in parallel with the completion of each phase of rank reform; specific ranks will only be eligible for the new salary scale once they have been restruc-tured. Candidates who are not selected have the option of either accepting a demotion, which would, under the new pay structure, still involve a significant rise in salary of up to 500%, or retiring and accepting a sever-ance package. Severance packages, which are expected to cost $5.6m, will offer one year's salary under the new salary scale, and an opportunity for vocational training.[141]

In July 2006, Karzai issued a decree calling for the acceleration of the reform process. The decree also authorised a 'rebalancing' of the police to address rising insecurity in the south.[142] The rebalancing, urged by the US and other donors, consisted of three measures: the disbanding of the highway police, the most corrupt branch of the ANP, and their integra-tion into the uniformed police and border police; the redeployment of

stand-by police battalions from the north to the south; and the recruitment and training of 2,100 temporary ANP personnel in support of the
stand-by battalions in the south.[143] In addition, the government announced
that it would recruit militia forces – the Afghan National Auxiliary Police
(ANAP) – to supplement the police.

Reform of the Interior Ministry
Reform of the Interior Ministry was perceived as secondary to overhauling
the police. This was exemplified by the fact that the GPPO embedded only
one senior adviser in the ministry, with a mandate to advance administrative and personnel reforms by late 2003.[144] In the aftermath of the Bonn
Conference, the Panjshiri faction of the Northern Alliance entrenched its
control over large parts of the Interior Ministry. While Jalali succeeded in
weakening the factional hold over the ministry during his tenure in 2003–
2005, he could not remove it.

The apparent reluctance to advance reform in the Interior Ministry
began to change, albeit slowly, with the entrance of the US into the police-
reform process in 2003. Although the US has continued to focus primarily
on police training, resources earmarked for the Interior Ministry have
steadily increased. In recognition of DynCorp's failure to make adequate
headway in advancing reform, the CSTC-A contracted MPRI, which
took responsibility for the reform process in 2006. MPRI's involvement is
intended to be temporary, until such time as DynCorp is able to recruit the
necessary expertise to reassume its role. In 2006, MPRI placed 15 mentors in
the Interior Ministry, with the purpose of replicating many of the systems
established in the Defence Ministry, covering areas such as personnel and
logistics management and legal affairs.[145] Most MPRI mentors have a dual
role advising in the development of systems and mentoring senior ministry staff.

A number of measures were taken in 2006 to expand the Interior
Ministry's command and control capacity. The first of five Regional
Command Centers (RCCs), intended to rationalise and formalise the chain
of command, was established in Kandahar, on the same site as the RTC.
With the exception of the Kabul RCC, all will initially be co-located with
RTCs to enable dual use of infrastructure, equipment and resources. The
five regional command areas mirror those of the ANA, a deliberate step
intended to ensure greater cooperation between the security forces.[146]
Meanwhile, a National Police Command Center opened in Kabul on 16
December 2006. The product of a $3.4m US-funded project, the facil-
ity 'enables a direct link and command and control with the five Afghan

National Police Regional Command Centers, as well as coordination with other agencies, such as the Ministry of Defence'.[147]

The Afghan National Auxiliary Police

The ANAP scheme calls for the mobilisation of 11,271 auxiliary police, to be deployed in 124 districts of 21 provinces, mainly in the south and east.[148] The purpose of the force is to secure static checkpoints and provide community policing, freeing up the regular police to conduct patrols and conduct counter-terrorist and counter-insurgency operations. Recruits for the force receive ten days' training, overseen by the CSTC-A in make-shift camps erected across the south and east.[149] The training focuses on community-policing skills. All ANAP recruits receive instruction in operational police techniques, as well as firearms and tactical training. They also receive classroom training on the Afghan constitution and ethics. Each camp is capable of producing 200 ANAP recruits every two weeks; 8,331 had completed training by July 2007.[150] All recruits are vetted through the vouching system employed by both the ANA and ANP; however, US trainers suspect that as many as one in ten of the new recruits 'is a Taliban agent'.[151] It is envisaged that ANAP recruits will receive additional training every quarter, which by the end of their first year will leave them with the same level of training as rank-and-file ANP patrolmen. This will permit the ANAP's integration into the regular police, enabling the ANP to meet its elevated force target of 82,000. However, US officials continue to refer to the programme as a 'temporary' or 'stop-gap' measure, and have little confidence in its suitability or sustainability.[152]

The plan also calls for the issuing of weapons to ANAP personnel, along with a uniform distinct from that of the regular police. Salaries will be identical with those of the ANP, and local ANP police commanders are meant to exert command and control over ANAP units. However, reports from the field indicate that the initial ANAP units have been issued with regular police uniforms and are not always commanded by ANP officers. In light of the fact that ANAP units are recruited, trained and deployed locally, they are vulnerable to factional manipulation. There are no clear accountability mechanisms to monitor and curb factional influence.[153]

While exploiting informal or traditional security structures to fill the prevailing security vacuum is surely a compelling idea, it may exacerbate insecurity. The plan is problematic in three ways. Firstly, the mobilisation of militias runs counter to the government's demilitarisation process and seems to undercut the Disbandment of Illegal Armed Groups (DIAG) programme. It has sent a powerful signal that the government is not committed to the demilitarisation process. Secondly, rearming and remobilising militias in Pashtun areas has prompted resentment among the northern ethnic factions, including the Tajiks, Uzbeks and Hazara, the majority of which have disarmed, at least partially, under the DDR programme. It has also aroused fears of resurgent Pashtun nationalism and exceptionalism, and has prompted many to warn of the prospect of remilitarisation.[154] Thirdly, without robust vetting, oversight and accountability structures, the ANAP could become another source of factionalism and corruption. It could serve as a convenient façade behind which factional commanders can maintain the integrity of their militias. Moreover, the force could, over time, become a rival to the ANP, hampering efforts to endow the regular police with a monopoly on the use of force.[155] Thus, a temporary mechanism intended to address short-term security needs could derail the police-reform process if it is not clearly situated within the formal security framework. Initial reports about the ANAP's performance have validated doubts about the force.[156]

Judicial reform

Reflecting on his experiences as High Representative for Bosnia-Herzegovina, Paddy Ashdown noted in a 2004 speech that:

> Crime and corruption follow swiftly in the footsteps of war, like a deadly virus. And if the rule of law is not established very swiftly, it does not take long before criminality infects every corner of its host, siphoning off the funds for re-construction, obstructing the process of stabilisation and corrupting every attempt to create decent government and a healthy civil society … This, above all was the mistake we made in Bosnia. We took six years to understand that the rule of law should have been the first thing. We are paying the price for that still.[157]

At the core of the endeavour to establish the rule of law in post-conflict societies are 'the legal norms and institutions necessary for the creation, interpretation, and application of the law'.[158] Although the police play an indispensable role in enforcing the law, 'without functioning courts and a judiciary system, there can be no rule of law'.[159] In Afghanistan, the international community and the Afghan government have failed to heed this axiom. Although the Bonn Agreement called for the appointment of a Judicial Reform Commission 'to rebuild the domestic justice system in accordance with Islamic principles, international standards, the rule of law and Afghan legal traditions', judicial reform was, from the outset, approached as a secondary objective to the task of training and equipping the country's security forces.[160] The wide disparity in international assistance provided to the security force train-and-equip programmes as compared to efforts to reconstitute the judicial system exemplify this prioritisation. According to the World Bank, only 3% of expenditures in the security sector were allocated to justice institutions in FY2003/04.[161] Given the decrepit state of the judicial system following the collapse of the Taliban, this level of assistance was grossly inadequate.

In a 2004 paper, J. Alexander Thier wrote that 'every aspect of a functioning judiciary is presently absent' in Afghanistan.[162] At the time, the judicial sector lacked physical infrastructure such as court houses, law libraries, prison facilities and office buildings for prosecutors and lawyers. Adequately trained jurists were in short supply; the majority of judges, for instance, lacked formal legal training. Finally, a complete record of the law had not been assembled and disseminated, creating regional variations in the nature and application of legal statutes. Despite programmes to address each of these areas, the situation had changed little by the beginning of 2007. In February 2007, the EU's External Relations Commissioner, Benita Ferrero-Waldner, affirmed that all of Afghanistan's judicial institutions 'are absolutely in urgent need of reform'. Ferrero-Waldner announced an EU pledge of €600m to help reform Afghanistan's public administration, 40% of which would be allocated to the judicial sector.[163]

The Afghan government's October 2005 judicial reform strategy, entitled *Justice for All*, affirmed that working conditions for state justice officials were inadequate, and recognised that, 'while significant progress had been made in equipping military and law enforcement units, almost nothing has been accomplished to provide resources for the justice system'.[164] One of the most conspicuous shortfalls concerns the lack of judicial buildings. In many parts of the country, judicial proceedings are conducted outdoors or in temporary structures like tents. International donors have assisted with repairs to the judicial infrastructure, but this has largely been ad hoc. As of June 2005, donors had funded the construction or rehabilitation of 45 judicial buildings, including 23 provincial courthouses, eight Justice Ministry and prosecutors' offices at the provincial level and 14 district court facilities.[165] USAID is engaged in rebuilding provincial judicial infrastructure, and Italy has funded renovations and repairs to the Justice Ministry building in Kabul, and the Faculty of Law and Political Science at Kabul University.[166] PRTs have also been involved in the refurbishment of district courthouses. International agencies have taken steps to provide justice actors with the materials and equipment they need for their duties, including office supplies, vehicles, telephones, furniture, computers and generators.

While some progress has been made in rebuilding judicial infrastructure at the national and provincial levels, little has been achieved at the district level, the main point of contact between Afghans and the judicial system. An EC-funded UNDP project, dubbed the Access to Justice at the District Level Program, was developed in late 2005 to address this problem. One component of the €6m, 30-month project is the refurbishment of the district-level judicial infrastructure. However, the resources allocated to the programme are far from adequate.

Human capacity is also limited. According to Ferrero-Waldner: 'the system is operating with staff who are insufficiently trained or educated – recruited through a system that is not at all transparent – and who do not operate under very credible mechanisms for [ensuring] accountability and discipline'.[167] A survey conducted by the Supreme Court with assistance from USAID, released in May 2006, found that a third of Afghanistan's 1,415 judges have no higher-education qualifications. Of those, 16.1% had been educated only at madrassas.[168] According to the survey, there were 400 vacant posts and a dearth of qualified candidates to fill them.[169]

Donors have funded a range of training programmes to improve the qualifications of existing judicial personnel and prepare the next generation of jurists. However, as with the reform experience elsewhere in the justice sector, these initiatives have been ad hoc and poorly coordinated. The first major training programme, called Interim Training for the Afghan Judiciary, was launched in July 2003. Implemented by the International Development Law Organization (IDLO), with funding from Italy, the programme provided 18 months of 'skills-oriented training' to 500 judges, prosecutors and Justice Ministry personnel. Since then, IDLO has implemented two other projects, funded by Italy and the Canadian International Development Agency (CIDA), providing additional specialised training to over 500 judges and 425 prosecutors, legal aid training for 50 law graduates from the University of Kabul and 20 women from the Ministry of Women's Affairs, training and technical assistance for members of the Faculty of Law and Political Science at Kabul University and training in legislative drafting for 240 government officials at the Secretariat for the National Assembly and the Justice Ministry.[170] The IDLO training programmes were strongly criticised by the Afghan government and by USAID. According to a senior official at the Justice Ministry, they were not based on comprehensive empirical analysis of the capacity needs of the justice system. Moreover, Afghanistan's permanent justice institutions – the Supreme Court, the Justice Ministry and the Attorney-General's office – were not adequately consulted over the design of the programmes. Indeed, the IDLO often overlooked or ignored Afghan concerns.[171]

Another Italian-led programme with a training focus is the Provincial Justice Initiative (PJI). The PJI provides targeted training for up to 50 jurists per province. By June 2006 the programme, which also provides vital equipment and materials such as computers, mobile phones and generators, had reached eight provinces. Its aim is to address between three and five provinces a year, allocating roughly $200,000 to each.[172]

Perhaps the most conspicuous failing of the training programmes has been their lack of a monitoring and evaluation component. There has been no follow-up training or assessments of whether graduates were applying their new knowledge. Monitoring undertaken by UNAMA's rule of law unit revealed that judges and prosecutors were 'not applying fair trial standards or properly implementing the interim criminal procedure code'.[173] To address such deficiencies and assert Afghan ownership over the training process, the Supreme Court established a Judicial Training and Education Committee to 'develop a more coordinated approach to the planning, implementation and evaluation of training programs'.[174] The committee oversees the implementation of an induction course for new judicial actors, and is working to develop a system of continuing education and training. Donors including USAID, Germany's GTZ and the Italian Justice Project provide assistance and technical support.[175] In the future, all continuing education is to be provided at the National Legal Training Center, established in Kabul in 2006 with Italian and US assistance.[176]

One of the legacies of Afghanistan's constantly shifting political terrain since 1964, with its numerous changes of regime, is a convoluted and overlapping body of law.[177] The Bonn Agreement recognised the 1964 constitution and all existing laws that were consistent with Afghanistan's international legal obligations. A subsequent presidential decree, issued in 2002, mandated the Justice Ministry to de-conflict the legal system, removing any contradictions between existing laws, and determine which laws were valid. A new constitution, endorsed in 2004, provided a foundation for the rationalisation of the country's legal framework. However, by the beginning of 2007 the process had made only limited progress.[178] Among the achievements of the law-reform process has been the passage of some essential legislation, such as the Law on the Organization and Jurisdiction of the Courts, the Juvenile Justice Code and the Law on Prisons and Detention Centers. The enactment of the Interim Criminal

Procedure Code in 2004 represents one of the more contentious aspects of the process. Drafted by Italian legal experts, the law, featuring 98 articles, was ostensibly written to meet the demands of the immediate post-conflict environment.[179] However, Afghan jurists have argued that the standards it sets are impractical in light of the human and institutional deficits in the system. For instance, prosecutors and the police have said that they lack the resources to meet the statutory timelines for detention, leading to their routine violation. The Afghan Attorney-General's office drafted a new code of criminal procedure, without international guidance, which it submitted to the other judicial institutions for consultation in April 2006.[180] Italy has complained that the new code fails to meet basic international standards, embodied in the 1976 International Covenant on Civil and Political Rights, to which Afghanistan is a signatory.[181]

Close scrutiny of the judicial-reform process in early 2007 shows that the obstacles to change remain formidable. One of the foremost of these obstacles, and a theme that runs throughout the SSR process, is coordination. Coordination has broken down at every level: between the main donors, between the government and the donors and among the government's main judicial institutions. The resultant lack of consensus on even the most fundamental aspects of the reform process prevented the formation of a coherent strategy until late 2005.

The Judicial Reform Commission established by the Bonn Agreement was intended to coordinate all the main stakeholders and ensure Afghan ownership. However, the 16-member commission was dissolved only three months after its creation. Ideological and political differences among its members, coupled with the lack of a clearly defined agenda, led to the commission's demise. A second Judicial Reform Commission, established in November 2002, was seen to be more professional and less overtly partisan, but was hindered by the same political turmoil that plagued its predecessor.[182] It survived until 2005, when it was disbanded. According to one USAID official, the very notion of an independent commission was flawed: 'the process cannot be taken out of the permanent institutions and determined by a group of wise men'.[183] Instead of nurturing genuine local ownership through careful consultations and consensus-building, the commission, comprised largely of Western Afghan expatriates commanding large consultancy fees, represented an attempt to import ownership and alienated Afghanistan's permanent justice institutions.

Perhaps the most problematic coordination failure pertains to the relationship between the two principal donors to the process, Italy and the US. Their differing legal traditions – Italy's civil-code system versus US common law – have been one of the main sources of division. Tensions between the two donors can also be attributed to the lead-nation system. Italy complained that the US, which by 2006 was the largest donor to the process, had usurped its lead-nation status. The system became redundant after the London Conference in 2006, which transferred lead responsibility from Italy to the Afghan government; however, Italy continued to see itself as the 'focal point' for the process.[184] The end of the lead-nation system in the justice sector, and the concomitant assertion of Afghan leadership of the process, gave new life to the Justice Sector Consultative Group (CG) as a mechanism to coordinate reforms.[185] The group is one of numerous CGs established under the auspices of the Finance Ministry to coordinate stakeholders around specific national programmes.[186] The CGs were subsequently recalibrated and realigned to conform with the structure of the Interim Afghan National Development Strategy (I-ANDS). Whereas the group served initially as 'a forum for foreigners', it has become increasingly effective as Afghan involvement has increased.[187]

The improved effectiveness of the CG structure can be attributed to better working relations between Afghanistan's permanent justice institutions, which had hitherto been strained. The relationship between the Supreme Court – the country's highest court, responsible for managing the entire court system – and the Justice Ministry was particularly problematic. In late 2005, a senior ministry official compared the Supreme Court, and particularly the then chief justice, Fazel Hady Shinwari, to a 'brick wall' blocking any meaningful reform. Shinwari's main goal was to maintain the status quo and ensure the primacy of sharia law over secular provisions of the constitution.[188] The appointment of Shinwari, who formerly headed a madrassa in Peshawar and who lacks secular legal training, represented part of a political deal made by Karzai with the conservative Islamic commander Abdul Rabb Rasul Sayyaf. Shinwari openly flouted provisions of the constitution, particularly pertaining to democratic rights and freedoms, and sought among other things to ban cable television and prevent women from singing and dancing in public.[189] In each case, the Supreme Court's rulings were ignored, but they nevertheless represented an overt attempt to instrumentalise the courts to impose a particularistic interpretation of Islam on Afghan society.

Concerns over the potential of the Supreme Court to subvert the constitution, notably the basic individual rights it enshrined, were eased in May 2006, when the new parliament rejected Shinwari's reappointment by a vote of 117 to 77. Opponents cited rampant corruption in the courts, Shinwari's lack of formal legal education and his fundamentalist views as reasons why he should not be reappointed.[190] Three other conservative appointees, all allies of Shinwari, were similarly voted down. In July 2006, parliament approved another slate of Supreme Court candidates viewed as progressive moderates. At the head of the list, as the new chief justice, was Abdul Salam Azimi, a moderate Islamic scholar and the primary drafter of Afghanistan's 2004 constitution.[191] The new court, inaugurated on 5 August 2006, is younger, dominated by highly educated technocrats trained in sharia and secular law, and devoid of links to fundamentalist circles.[192] In his first six months in office Azimi dismissed or jailed eight judges and four clerks for corruption and led a review of 6,000 cases that have been challenged. He also spearheaded the establishment of a new accountability system, requiring provincial judges to submit comprehensive reports on their cases.[193]

Another obstacle to reform was the lack of an overarching strategy, a by-product of the coordination problems among the main actors. Italy designed a strategy early in the process, but it was not endorsed by the other stakeholders due to a lack of adequate Afghan input. It was not until late 2005 that a coherent strategy materialised. In August 2005, a three-day conference called 'Justice for All' was held in Kabul to consult all the main stakeholders in the process – the permanent justice institutions, Afghan legal scholars, UN agencies, donors, NGOs and civil-society groups – on the 'dimensions of reform, benchmarks and timelines'.[194] The result of the conference was a ten-year strategic framework of the same name, finalised by the permanent justice institutions with assistance from the Justice Sector Consultative Group and released on 25 October 2005. This divided the process into five parts: reforming the law, making judicial institutions effective, reaching out to the Afghan public, consulting with the community on traditional justice and cooperation with other government programmes.[195] For each dimension, the framework identifies succinct goals and benchmarks to be achieved in three time horizons: 1–3 years, 4–5 years and 5–10 years. Like the inauguration of the new Supreme Court, the introduction of the strategy was a watershed for the judicial-reform process, endowing it with greater direction and purpose and improving coordination.

One critical area addressed by the strategy, which had hitherto been largely ignored in the formal reform process, was the issue of the traditional or informal justice system. The framework recognised that traditional institutions deal with up to 90% of 'legal matters' in the country.[196] A survey conducted by the Asia Foundation in 2006, the largest ever undertaken in Afghanistan, found that only 16% of Afghans take legal disputes to government courts.[197] Rather, they look to traditional structures like the *jirga*, *maraca* and *shura*.[198] These local structures rely on a fusion of customary law, indigenous cultural norms and sharia law. The formal justice system is perceived across much of Afghanistan as expensive, corrupt, elitist, inefficient and distant. As Wardak states: 'these traditional institutions of popular justice ... resolved tribal disputes and local conflicts expeditiously and in a cost-effective way'.[199] However, 'some of these traditional practices violate Afghan and international law, including honour killings, forced and underage marriage, and payment of blood money in lieu of punishment'.[200]

The government has been reluctant to cede authority or grant legitimacy to informal or traditional legal mechanisms, taking the view that recognition of such structures would erode the power of the formal legal system and the state. Yet it may also be the case that the establishment of 'a competent, coherent and effective justice system as a central component of a legitimate Afghan state ... need not ... [be] at the expense of all traditional or informal dispute resolution mechanisms'. A positive relationship between the informal and formal systems may instead 'enable the government to harness the good of [the informal] system, while also working to curtail its most problematic aspects'.[201] Finding this equilibrium, as the *Justice for All* strategy recognises, requires work to 'further study, dialogue and develop policy on the relationship between customary and "formal" law'.[202] A number of studies have been undertaken to define, map and analyse the informal system.[203] One of the overarching conclusions to emerge is that the 'formal and informal already co-exist, and will do so for many years to come. The question is whether they will co-exist in a cooperative or antagonistic environment'.[204]

Any reform of the justice system, and the civil service in general, will be fruitless without efforts to address endemic corruption. In August 2006, Karzai assigned the attorney-general to 'crack down, arrest and prosecute the perpetrators of corruption in the Government at all offices'. In asking the attorney-general to take 'decisive action', Karzai urged him to address the problem even if it reached 'high levels of government'.[205] The most obvious starting point is the justice sector itself, the natural vanguard against graft in the state but, in Afghanistan, one of the most corrupt sectors of government.

As with the police, high levels of corruption in the judiciary can be attributed partly to low rates of pay for jurists; the average judge in Afghanistan earns approximately $50 per month, an eighth of what a police colonel makes under the ANP salary structure launched in 2006.[206] The principal mechanism to overhaul the judicial administration and rationalise personnel and salary schemes is the Afghan government's Public Administration Reform programme (PAR). Overseen by the Independent Administrative Reform and Civil Service Commission (IARCSC), with support from the World Bank and other donors, the programme aims to 'provide an efficient, effective, and transparent civil service'.[207] One of the central components of the PAR is the Priority Reform and Restructuring programme (PRR), which is intended to reshape and rationalise administrative structures and lines of authority, introduce a new pay and grading system and ensure the application of merit-based recruitment and promotion criteria.[208] By the end of 2005, 3,000 jobs in the justice sector had been reclassified and opened up to merit-based recruitment in the justice sector, a precondition for a raise in the salary scale. According to the *Justice for All* strategy, the process needs to be extended to about 20,000 jobs in the permanent justice institutions.[209] The process has developed slowly, and has faced particular difficulties in implementing and enforcing the merit-based appointment system. As a senior Justice Ministry official explained, the PRR is a well-designed mechanism, but it has not worked in practice.[210] It will have to be reinvigorated if it is to force through the administrative changes needed to make good on the government's ambitious commitments to tackle corruption.

The prison system

The rule of law system can be conceptualised as a triad with three points: the police, the judiciary and the prison system. The third of these is clearly the most under-resourced element in Afghanistan. This is perhaps not surprising, as prisons are not generally an attractive target for donor funding. In fact, many donors place restrictions on their aid that prevent its use on prisons. However, given the decrepit state of the Afghan prison system, the shortfall in funding has been both conspicuous and debilitating, making progress in the other two elements of the rule of law system difficult.

Two countrywide surveys, conducted by the International Committee of the Red Cross (ICRC) and the CFC-A, reveal a prison system that is chronically overcrowded and lacks basic amenities such as sanitation and medical facilities. Many prisons are in such a dilapidated state that they are uninhabitable.[211] Of the 34 provincial prisons under the control of the Central Prison Directorate (CPD), most require urgent repairs and refurbishment to bring them up to international standards.[212] The poor conditions of Afghanistan's prisons were demonstrated in 2006, when hundreds of inmates at Pul-i Charki prison in Kabul, the best-funded and best-maintained prison in the country, went on hunger strike over the poor treatment they had received. The prison warden and eight staff were subsequently removed by the attorney-general, a sign that the government was taking the appalling situation of its prisons more seriously.[213] With the prison population increasing rapidly – from 600 in 2001 to 6,085[214] in January 2006 – the need for reform is urgent.[215]

Authority over the prison system was transferred from the Interior Ministry to the Justice Ministry in 2003. However, it was not until the promulgation in May 2005 of the Prisons and Detention Act that the CPD was formally integrated into the Justice Ministry.[216] Italy, by virtue of its lead-nation status in the justice sector, has been one of the principal funders of reform initiatives, but has lacked the resources to imbue the process with the momentum it requires. The limited progress that has been made has largely been confined to prison renovations in Kabul. UNODC has been the main implementing body for reforms, with funding from Italy, Canada, the UK and Belgium. Renovations at Pul-i Charki prison include the construction of a closed women's facility and the establish-ment of a maximum-security unit for high-profile drug offenders. The UN Children's Fund (UNICEF) is overseeing the construction of a juvenile facility.[217] In 2006, building work began on two new regional prison facili-ties, each costing $6m, in Mazar-i Sharif and Gardez. Funded by Italy and contracted to the UN Office for Project Services (UNOPS), both facilities are to have a capacity of approximately 450 inmates.[218] Many PRTs have also undertaken ad hoc repairs of prison and detention facilities in their areas of operation, but these are only short-term solutions.

Given the culture of abuse that prevails at prisons across the country, staff training is also necessary to ensure that the fundamental rights of prisoners are upheld. The CPD employs approximately 9,000 staff, 250 in Kabul, 4,500 in provincial facilities and 4,000 in small district-level facili-ties.[219] Personnel, mainly former police or militia fighters, have not been provided with specialised training and are frequently inadequately paid. To address this problem, the CPD has established a Central Training Facility (CTF) in the grounds of the Pul-i Charki prison. The US Corrections Sector Support Program (CSSP) has established a project to develop a national training programme for existing personnel, featuring a four-week course for rank-and-file staff and a ten-week course for officers. The programme, which would offer training at the CTF and at least three regional centres, began in May 2006 with a train-the-trainers course.[220]

The reform process is overseen by the Consultative Working Group on Prisons and Detention Centres, chaired by the Ministry of Justice and under the umbrella of the Justice Sector Consultative Group. While the body, which includes representation from UNODC, UNAMA, the JSSP, Italy and other donors, has become increasingly cohesive and effective over time, the sector continues to lack a wider strategic plan and resources remain inadequate.

By 2006, there was almost universal recognition among Afghan and international actors of the deleterious impact of the slow pace of judicial and prison reform on the SSR and wider state-building processes. Yet despite this realisation the process continues to face resource shortfalls. While many donors have augmented their support to judicial institutions, their contributions remain incommensurate with the scale of the challenges that exist. The Afghan government estimates that the justice-sector reform process could face a shortfall of $1bn over the coming decade.[221] Compared to the vast sums being spent on training and equipping the police and army, this is a modest sum. Increasing EU engagement in the process will help to address this shortfall, but larger and more long-term funding commitments are needed to enable the government to meet the benchmarks and goals encapsulated in the *Justice for All* strategy.

Demilitarisation

While the military, police and judicial reform pillars of the SSR agenda have sought to transform the institutions of the state, the DDR pillar endeavours to confront the legacy of past conflict in the form of tens of thousands of combatants and the proliferation of millions of weapons. Experience in post-conflict settings elsewhere shows that, until armed groups and individual ex-combatants are demobilised and reintegrated into society and illicit weapons collected or destroyed, new institutions will remain vulnerable to distortion or collapse. In a 2003 speech, Karzai asserted that 'achieving DDR answers the deepest aspirations of the Afghan people, who are eager to move away from war and violence toward a peaceful, safe and civil society'.[222] Karzai was speaking at a conference organised in Tokyo by the Japanese government to provide a forum for the Afghan government to present its plans for reforming the security sector. Although the original focus of the pillar was on establishing a DDR programme for the AMF, it subsequently grew to encompass an initiative to disband illegal armed groups outside the AMF. Despite a slow start, by 2007 the demilitarisation process was widely regarded as a success for the SSR process. However, although the numerical achievements are certainly impressive, closer examination shows that progress has been tenuous.

Table 1 **ANBP Funding Breakdown**	
Donor	**Contribution (USD)**
Japan	91 million
UK	19 million
Canada	16 million
USA	9 million
The Netherlands	4 million
The European Commission	1.9 million
Norway	0.8 million
Switzerland	0.5 million
TOTAL	**142.2 million**

Source: Afghanistan New Beginnings Programme (ANBP), *Afghanistan New Beginnings Programme*, Brochure for the second Tokyo conference on Consolidation of Peace in Afghanistan (Kabul: ANBP, 15 June 2006), p. 5.

The Disarmament, Demobilisation and Reintegration of Former Combatants
The 2003 Tokyo conference was attended by more than 30 donor countries, as well as the EU and ten international organisations. Out of it came the Afghan New Beginnings Programme (ANBP), a DDR project implemented by UNDP on behalf of the Afghan government. Formally launched in April 2003, the stated objective of the ANBP, which focused solely on active units of the AMF, was:

> To decommission formations and units up to a total of 100,000 officers and soldiers and in the process to collect, store and deactivate weapons currently in their possession in order to be able to reconstruct the Afghan National Army (ANA) and return those not required to civilian life.[223]

While disarmament was explicitly stated as a central goal, in practice it was treated as a peripheral aspect. The two underlying goals of the process were 'to break the historic patriarchical [*sic*] chain of command existing between the former commanders and their men; and to provide the demobilized personnel with the ability to become economically independent'.[224] The Afghan government and the ANBP initially estimated that 100,000 combatants were eligible to enter the DDR process. This figure represented a compromise between the Afghan Defence Ministry, which initially claimed that there were more than 250,000 AMF soldiers on duty, and UNAMA, which asserted that there were only 45,000–50,000 ex-combatants.[225] No comprehensive assessment of the scale and nature of the problem was conducted to inform the programme's design, and ANBP officials were

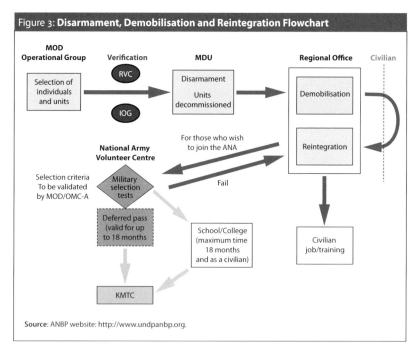

Figure 3: Disarmament, Demobilisation and Reintegration Flowchart

Source: ANBP website: http://www.undpanbp.org.

forced to rely on figures provided by the Defence Ministry. However, the ministry and AMF commanders had an interest in overstating the number of troops under their command, as they could claim more resources from the central government to feed, house and remunerate them. After a year of operation, the ANBP lowered the operational target to approximately 60,000, concluding that a large proportion of the AMF personnel on the payroll of the Defence Ministry were in fact 'ghost soldiers'.

The minimum requirements for entry into the $142m (see Table 1) programme were eight months of military service and the submission of a functioning weapon, as determined by an ANBP weapons expert.[226] This prerequisite was largely symbolic, and intended to demonstrate the individual soldier's commitment to peace. The programme does not contain a mechanism to verify that individual soldiers or commanders are submitting all of their weapons stocks, or to compel them to do so.

After weapons collection in a particular area was completed, ex-soldiers were directed to the ANBP regional office for demobilisation, where they were presented with a list of employment or educational options. Ex-combatants were offered a choice of several reintegration packages devised by the ANBP in cooperation with the Afghan government and international partner organisations. If no immediate opportunities could be identified, or if the agricultural package could not begin for seasonal reasons, the ANBP offered temporary wage-labour positions until suitable alternatives could be made available.[227]

The main phase of the programme, launched in May 2004, proceeded slowly during its first three months of operation, primarily because of obstruction by commanders and insecurity. The process began to achieve tangible results in the latter part of 2004, due to two factors. Firstly, the Political Parties Law promulgated on 18 October 2003 provided a powerful incentive for armed factions with political ambitions to comply with the DDR process.[228] The law prohibits political parties from having 'military organizations or affiliations with armed forces', a principle also enshrined in the constitution, and allows for the dissolution of parties that transgress this statute.[229] Intent on registering candidates in time for the October 2004 presidential elections, factional groups sought to demonstrate their support for the DDR process by demobilising elements of their militias. The increased level of cooperation exhibited by all the main factional groups, although short of full compliance, was a product of their political ambitions and determination to avoid complications in the registration process.[230] Secondly, in the run-up to the presidential elections, the US deepened its engagement in the process, applying pressure on recalcitrant commanders to comply. The shift in the US approach, which had previously been characterised by ambivalence and even obstructionism, was intended to boost Karzai's electoral fortunes and address deteriorating security conditions.

Commanders manipulated the process in particular regions, arbitrarily choosing candidates for entry into the programme and pilfering reintegration assistance.[231] In an attempt to address commander obstructionism, the ANBP launched a Commander Incentive Program (CIP) in 2004. The central component of the scheme was a redundancy package which provided commanders with a $550–$650 monthly cash stipend for a two-year period, in exchange for their cooperation with the ANBP. For commanders unlikely to be enticed by financial incentives alone, opportunities for travel and training overseas (primarily in Japan) and the prospect of a government posting were offered to suitable candidates, as determined by the government and ANBP.[232] The two-year, $5m programme, funded by Japan, targeted 550 militia commanders across the country, 460 of whom had entered the programme by June 2006.[233] The redundancy payments continued until June 2007, with the programme scheduled to reach its conclusion the following September.[234]

The disarmament and demobilisation phase of the process formally came to an end on 7 July 2005. It saw the demobilisation of 63,380 ex-combatants and the collection of 57,629 light and medium weapons. The programme also led to the 'de-financing' of 100,000 soldiers – denoting the formal removal of soldiers, both real and 'ghost', from the state payroll – resulting in savings of $120m a year.[235] In the light of the challenges faced by the programme, its accomplishments are certainly impressive. However, many militia networks have remained intact, and it would be premature to deliver a final verdict on the programme until the impact of its reintegration component is adequately assessed.

The fundamental goal of DDR was to permanently break down military formations, severing the patronage-based links between commanders and their militiamen. Reintegration programming, including vocational training, small-business support and agricultural packages,[236] may have provided the basic tools for former combatants to re-enter civilian life; however, it is unclear whether the entry points into the civilian economy will exist to enable beneficiaries to exploit these tools over the medium and long term. With economic activity in many areas of the country stagnant and unemployment hovering around 25–30%, ex-combatants could be forced back into militias.[237]

In an effort to gauge the impact of the reintegration process, the ANBP launched a Client Evaluation Survey in 2006 that interviewed 5,000 programme beneficiaries who had received at least 6–9 months of reintegration assistance.[238] The survey showed that 93% of respondents were satisfied with the reintegration assistance that they received, and 90% were still employed.[239] What the survey did not show was whether these positive results were sustainable, or whether the ex-combatants could withstand natural fluctuations in the economy. Most importantly, will they be able to endure the inevitable scaling down of international aid, which has provided a steady stream of labour-intensive projects to absorb ex-combatants? To ensure that former fighters do not fall back into previous patterns of military mobilisation, continuous long-term support is required from a permanent government body. Plans have been introduced to build the capacity of key ministries, such as Labour and Social Affairs and Agriculture, to 'deliver reintegration services over the long-term' to former combatants.[240] One such plan envisages the integration of some of the structures of the ANBP into a special branch of the Ministry of Labour and Social Affairs.[241]

The Disbandment of Illegal Armed Groups (DIAG)

A glaring shortcoming of the DDR programme was its singular focus on officers and soldiers within the formal structure of the AMF. This ignored informal militia groups. Afghanistan's illegal armed groups range from tribal self-defence forces, primarily found in the southeast (known as *arbakai*), to criminal gangs.[242] The failure to target these groups from the outset of the process allowed them to solidify their power bases and consolidate their control over vital sources of revenue, such as the drug trade. The success of many AMF commanders in shielding their units from the DDR process necessitated a further round of disarmament. As the DIAG strategy document affirms, 'several groups who entered the AMF and were formally demobilized through the DDR program retained in many cases their core staff and a substantial amount of light weapons ... [and] a number of commanders retained control of armed groups through their position as governors, chiefs of police and other local official positions'.[243] The threat these illegal armed groups pose to the state is multifaceted: they collect illegal taxes, obstructing government revenue collection; they are involved in the illegal exploitation of natural resources – oil, gas, coal and gemstones – and in some cases have assumed control of state-owned industries; they subvert reform processes and intimidate local-government officials and security forces; and they drive the illegal economy, most notably the drug trade.[244]

In February 2005, as the formal DDR programme entered its final phase, the ANBP was authorised, with funding from the Canadian government, to begin planning a programme to disband illegal armed groups. A planning cell was established within the ANBP to collect intelligence and, in conjunction with the government and a range of international stakeholders, to devise an approach to address the problem. The planning cell estimated that there were 1,870 illegal armed groups[245] in the country, comprising roughly 129,000 militiamen.[246] The government has conservatively estimated that these groups possess 336,000 small arms and light weapons, 56,000 of which are believed to have been concealed from the DDR process by the AMF. The actual number is likely to be much higher, considering the scale of previous arms transfers into the country and the size of illegal weapons caches uncovered by Coalition, ISAF and government security forces since 2001.

While the DDR process was internationally driven, the Disbandment of Illegal Armed Groups (DIAG) programme is government led. The Demobilisation and Reintegration Commission acts as the DIAG steering committee,[247] the high-level policy lead for the process, giving it strategic direction and coordinating the various actors engaged in it. The ANBP provides technical assistance and expertise to the Joint Secretariat and the DIAG Provincial Committees, the main Afghan bodies implementing the process.[248] The designated end-state for the programme is the disarmament and disbanding of all 'identifiable illegal armed groups'. Although it was originally envisioned that the programme would reach its conclusion by the end of 2007, by the latter half of 2007 it was still at an early stage.[249] The programme was originally estimated to cost $11m, with another $35m earmarked for community-development projects, but the final cost is likely to be much higher. The bulk of the funding has come from the Japanese government.[250]

The process can be broken down into three phases: voluntary compliance, negotiated compliance and enforced compliance. The first phase involves fostering conditions conducive to voluntary compliance. Compliance is defined as the submission of 70% of the estimated weapons of the illegally armed group being targeted.[251] However, unlike the DDR programme there is no prescription that the weapons submitted meet a certain standard of functionality. Ex-combatants are informed of their legal obligations to disarm, and provided with a 30-day amnesty period in which to comply. Community and religious leaders will be used as intermediaries to encourage commanders to cooperate with the process. The prospect of development incentives in exchange for disarmament will be introduced to local communities as a means of placing pressure on militiamen and their commanders. While many observers have likened the DIAG programme to a weapons-for-development scheme such as that pioneered in Albania, the Afghan government has sought to dispel this notion. The *Guidelines for DIAG Development Activities* state that 'development projects shall not be considered as direct incentives to, or rewards for, disarmament, but may serve as a motivation for the community (*shuras*, leaders) to persuade the illegal armed groups to disarm and disband'.[252] The government is keen to avoid incentivising the illegal possession of arms, opting instead to emphasise the obligation of armed groups to disarm under state law.

Phase two comes into effect after 30 days, when the designated period for voluntary compliance expires. It involves multi-track negotiation at the national and provincial levels as well as through local actors such as village mullahs and local *shuras*. Public-information efforts will be intensified, with a focus on the implications of non-compliance, notably the denial of access to community-development funds. When the negotiation period expires, the enforcement phase comes into effect. The mandate for enforcing the process falls on the Interior Ministry and the ANP. In extreme circumstances, the ANA and international security forces could be called in to assist.

The DIAG process was launched on a limited scale in late 2005. During its early stages the process targeted specific actors: government officials and national assembly and provincial council election candidates with links to illegal armed groups. The government sought to use the leverage provided by government positions and candidatures in the legislative elections to place pressure on militias to comply with the DIAG process. Although only achieving limited success,[253] these initiatives paved the way for the main stage of the process, launched on 1 May 2006 in Kapeesa province, where 38 commanders were issued notices instructing them to submit their weapons within the standard 30-day period. The process had an inauspicious beginning, foreshadowing future problems, as only seven weapons had been submitted by the end of the 30-day voluntary period.[254] As of June 2006, the DIAG process had engaged 1,275 illegal armed groups, and by July 2007 it had collected 31,484 weapons. However, the bulk of these weapons, a fraction of the estimated amount in circulation, were collected in ad hoc voluntary submissions prior to the launch of the main stage, and only 40% were categorised as usable. Illegal armed groups are giving the impression of cooperation by dumping their unserviceable equipment, concealing their best weapons for use or sale on the illicit weapons market. The poor performance of the DIAG programme in its initial months of operation almost led to its termination in mid 2006. In the words of one official working on the programme, 'DIAG nearly died' due to the disappointing early results of the main stage.[255]

The DIAG process has failed to achieve its goals due in large part to a lack of political will from the government. The most conspicuous example of the government's fragile commitment to the process is the large number of government officials who have maintained links with illegal armed groups. High-profile government ministries, even those directly involved in the DIAG process, have obstructed and even subverted the process. The executive branch, rather than championing the concept across the government, has sought to provide protection for government officials targeted by it. According to an official from the DIAG Joint Secretariat, the main implementing body for the programme, the government issued instructions not to pursue officials at the governor or cabinet level.[256] Several cabinet ministers, governors and parliamentarians appear on the list of the top ten illegal armed groups in the country compiled by the Joint Secretariat. Until serious attempts are made to persuade these figures to disarm, the process will remain paralysed.

The wholesale lack of compliance in many areas where the programme was applied shows how difficult it is to engage commanders effectively. The programme's designers erroneously assumed that the provision of development incentives would alienate communities from local commanders, thereby placing pressure on them to disarm. While this may be the case with community militias or self-defence forces, which are organic extensions of the local community, it is unlikely to affect criminal groups, whose interests diverge from local actors. Many militia groupings are already alienated from local communities due to their predatory behaviour, limiting the pressure that communities can bring to bear, and their involvement in the immensely profitable illicit economy makes community-development projects unattractive. Weapons provide criminal groups an entry ticket into the illicit economy; getting them to abandon their arms will require tailored individualised incentives, which the DIAG programme eschews. The same problem during the early stages of the DDR programme resulted in the establishment of the Commander Incentive Program. It is clear that the government may have to consider providing targeted incentives to groups to secure their engagement in the DIAG process. Of course, such an incentive framework will have perverse effects if it is not buttressed by credible and robust disincentives in the form of coercion by the security forces. Even on this score, it is unlikely that the government has the capacity or the political will to forcibly disarm uncooperative groups. Despite non-compliance by targeted groups during all stages of the process the government had, as of mid 2007, yet to employ force as dictated by the programme.

Significant advances have been made in the demilitarisation pillar between 2002 and 2007, but it would be premature to regard the process as a success, and important challenges remain. Although the DDR process succeeded in formally decommissioning the AMF, militia patronage networks have remained intact and the sustainability of the reintegration process is far from assured. For its part, the DIAG programme has engaged a large number of illegal armed groups, but has fully dissolved few and collected only a fraction of their weapons.

*   *   *

Considering the omnipresence of the SSR concept in Afghanistan in 2007, which is seen by many as the key to the success of the state-building project, it seems astonishing that, in 2001, the process was not viewed with particular urgency and was severely under-resourced. This false start was a result of the international community's failure to adequately grasp the extent and complexity of the security problem in Afghanistan following the Taliban's fall. According to a paper produced by the Afghan Office for the National Security Council (ONSC) ahead of the 2004 Berlin donor conference, initial planning for SSR was informed by international assessments that 'naively assumed an improvement in security which has not materialised'.[257] Attempts to compensate for this lost time skewed the SSR agenda. With donor states unwilling to contribute the international troop numbers needed to stabilise the country, SSR increasingly came to be seen as the answer to the rising tide of insecurity. The process became increasingly 'securitised', as the goal of training and equipping the security forces to get them 'into the fight' superseded all other priorities, particularly the 'soft' security elements of the process, such as judicial reform.[258] Rather than jumpstarting the process, this strategy created new bottlenecks and obstacles to reform.

By 2006, donors had recognised many of the gaps and problems in the process – from the acute under-resourcing of judicial reform to the issue of fiscal sustainability – and had augmented their investments. However, despite increased funding, primarily from the US, the process is still hampered by short-termism, exemplified by the introduction of the ANAP, a temporary mechanism that could undermine the demilitarisation and police-reform processes over the long term.

The related issues of coordination and ownership continued to hinder the SSR process in 2007. Although the lead-nation framework was ostensibly dissolved following the 2006 London conference, a development that has been welcomed by most stakeholders in the process, it was expanding US control over the SSR agenda that rendered the system obsolete. By early 2007, the US had become the largest financial contributor to four out of the five pillars, vastly outspending the existing lead donors in each. While increased US engagement has given the process a major boost, America's penchant for quick fixes, achieved by saturating problem areas with aid, could prove counterproductive.

Insufficient resources are not the only problem afflicting the process. For instance, Karzai has not always shown the political will necessary to address factionalisation and corruption in the security institutions, a by-product of his accommodationist leadership approach. Dedicating vast resources to a system when the commitment of the political leadership to the fundamental principles of the process is tenuous is not only wasteful, but could also exacerbate instability. Channelling increased funds into unreformed institutions can have the effect of increasing corruption, which will in turn alienate the population. This cycle can only be halted with genuine local commitment to reform, to de-factionalising and depoliticising the security system. The increase in attention and resources to the SSR process, particularly the security forces, over the past two years may succeed in addressing some blatant deficiencies in the security sector, but durable and sustainable change can only be achieved through the adoption of a holistic approach that aims to change the culture and ethos of the system. Achieving this change in vision requires a long-term approach by donors and Afghan stakeholders, and a genuine commitment to change.

CONCLUSION

The security environment in Afghanistan has steadily deteriorated since the overthrow of the Taliban regime in 2001, plumbing new depths with each passing year. This growing crisis can partially be attributed to missed opportunities at the outset of the state-building process. Opportunities were not taken to deal with some of the underlying drivers of conflict. Even as resource levels have increased after successive donor conferences, Afghan government and international responses to this adverse situation have been incommensurate with the scale and extent of the problem. But the problem facing Afghanistan is more than a lack of resources. There is a fundamental tension in the state-building agenda between short-term and long-term objectives, with a short-termist approach often prevailing. In the security sphere, this has translated into a conflict between strategies of short-term containment and stabilisation and long-term sustainable peace-building.

Many of the policies and practices of the Afghan government and the international community have been geared more to containing instability and insecurity than to resolving their underlying causes. Karzai's policy of accommodation towards some of Afghanistan's warlords; the US-led Coalition's employment of militia proxies in the south; and the prioritisation of security-force operational effectiveness above considerations of justice and governance are but a few examples of this approach. While security may improve in the short and medium term as a result of such strategies and tactics, new sources of instability may be created over the long term.

The US approach to Afghanistan in the first stages of the state-building process typifies this focus on immediate stabilisation and containment. The US mission, which rejected the nation-building paradigm, was geared first and foremost to destroying al-Qaeda and preventing Afghanistan from once again becoming a sanctuary for terrorists, rather than consolidating a certain type of peace. Preventing Afghanistan's instability from spilling over into the region and threatening the United States, as it did on 11 September 2001, was the primary objective. Over time, US policymakers came to the conclusion that only through state-building could that objective actually be achieved; however, critical time was lost.

State-building demands an appropriate balance between short-term and long-term considerations. While the Afghan process has been heavily skewed towards short-term objectives, some progress had been achieved by 2006 in striking a better balance. The London conference in January–February 2006 was a watershed in this regard, as it resulted in a comprehensive and integrated strategy for the country's reconstruction, the Afghanistan Compact, and new long-term donor commitments. In the security sphere, a number of signs in 2006 showed that the country may be moving away from the paradigm of containment to one of sustainable peace-building. The expansion of NATO forces across the country, particularly in the south, and the allocation of increased resources to the SSR process, including its soft components like justice, illustrated this shift. This influx of resources is critical, but must be accompanied by renewed political will to address some of the remaining obstacles to stability, such as the relationship with Pakistan, the presence of warlords and spoilers in the government and the drug trade. Until the international community convinces Pakistan to rein in cross-border militant activity and halt any clandestine support from its military and intelligence apparatus for the Taliban; until the Afghan government can challenge the dominance of commanders in the public administration and improve governance; and until the Afghan government and donors can resolve the contradictions in the counter-narcotics strategy, implementing a genuinely holistic approach featuring both comprehensive rural development and law enforcement, security will remain elusive.

A historic opportunity to transform Afghanistan in the wake of the Taliban's fall is slipping away as public disillusionment with the post-Taliban political order grows. To confront the emergent crisis of legitimacy, the Afghan government and the international community must re-examine their approach in the security sphere. The focus should be shifted from containing insecurity and safeguarding the regime to providing security, the rule of law and good governance to Afghans, whether in Kabul or in remote rural areas. In essence, this involves a fundamental shift in strategy, from one rooted in regime security to one focused on human security. Only when the government can provide the basic public goods of security and justice will it be able to defeat the insurgency and assert its sovereignty over the entire country. The government's failure to do this has prompted many Afghans, particularly in the south and east, to speak nostalgically of the Taliban, not due to any ideological affinity but because of the group's history of delivering security.

Achieving this shift in strategy will necessitate some difficult choices by donors and the Afghan government, choices that they have often been unwilling to make. It will require donors to remain committed to the country for a long time to come. It will demand a new emphasis on security-sector reform, to reinvigorate the process and transform it from a train-and-equip programme into a process capable of remaking the culture of the security apparatus. The challenge that faces the process is daunting – to remove the underlying public perception that the security forces and judiciary are predatory, alien and corrupt. SSR is not merely about creating security forces capable of protecting the central government from spoilers. It is also about building public faith in the security system. The process has made important strides, but it has only scratched the surface of the problem. It is clear that the Afghan security forces will be incapable of securing the entire national territory for some time to come, exemplifying the need for NATO's continued engagement.

Not only are NATO forces playing a vital role in combating the growing Taliban threat, but they are also making significant contributions to the SSR process through their involvement in in-service training for the security forces. It is clear that a significant NATO force presence will be required in Afghanistan for up to a decade, a reality that is unpalatable in NATO capitals, where electorates have become increasingly weary of the extended Afghan mission. The only way to expedite the withdrawal of international troops is by guaranteeing the success of SSR, which offers the only viable exit strategy for the international community. A premature exit by NATO forces would be likely to trigger the slow collapse of the post-Taliban political dispensation and the return of internecine conflict.

Endowing the Afghan state with the capacity to address the human security needs of the Afghan people is not solely an issue of resources and the provision of technical assistance. The failures of the SSR process have demonstrated that the principal challenges are political. Broadly speaking, the problem is one of political will. Karzai has been averse to removing political allies ensconced in the security institutions that have either obstructed reforms or been a major source of corruption. Such reluctance to upset the political balance stems partially from suspicions over the durability of the international commitment to the country. Karzai is unwilling to create splits in the political fabric when he is unsure how long the international community will buttress his administration. It is clear that donors cannot remain divorced from the political dimensions of the SSR process, whether it is reassuring the Afghan government of the longevity of its commitment or utilising conditionality arrangements on assistance to ensure greater adherence to key reforms.

Afghans must be in charge of the reform of their security institutions and the design and execution of the country's security policy. Executive and legislative bodies mandated to direct and provide oversight of the security sector, whether they are parliamentary commissions or the National Security Council, must be supported to ensure the accountability of the sector. International military actors must also show greater sensitivity to Afghan demands for increased input into military operations, especially in the light of the spate of civilian casualties in 2007 that has stoked Afghan resentment of the foreign military presence. However, while local ownership is an inviolable principle of state-building practice, the Afghan government is still far from self-sufficient in the security sphere. Endemically low levels of institutional and human capacity, high levels of corruption and criminality and scarce resources ensure that direct international engagement and support will be needed for the foreseeable future.

The international community must slowly devolve security responsibility to the Afghan government. Donors must avoid the temptation to do it for the Afghans, creating parallel institutional structures – staffed by international military personnel, aid workers, diplomats and consultants – that bypass the Afghan administration to undertake key security tasks. This is a common state-building practice that has undermined efforts to build Afghan capacity and develop the legitimacy of the fledgling government. International assistance will remain crucial for at least a decade, but it is the manner in which that assistance is delivered that is of paramount importance. Aid should take the form of capacity-building, embedded technical assistance and internationally monitored trust funds to channel funds through Afghan institutions in an accountable manner. The international community must avoid handing over security responsibility to the Afghan state before it is capable of handling that burden, otherwise it could collapse under the security and political pressures that prevail in the country. The uncomfortable reality for donors is that, even with a significant increase in support for the Afghan state-building project, conditions are likely to get worse before they get better. There is no quick fix. Some developments in 2006 and 2007 have renewed hopes that the government and donors possess the resolve to consolidate the impressive gains that have been made, but there is much still to do.

Introduction

1   Islamic Republic of Afghanistan, *Implementation of the Afghanistan Compact: Bi-Annual JCMB Report* (Kabul: Islamic Republic of Afghanistan, November 2006), p. 2.

2   International Crisis Group (ICG), *Afghanistan's Endangered Compact*, Asia Briefing No. 59 (Brussels: ICG, 29 January 2007), p. 8.

3   Islamic Republic of Afghanistan, *Implementation of the Afghanistan Compact*, p. 2.

4   Integrated Regional Information Network (IRIN), Afghanistan, *UN Highlights Conflict's Impact on Civilians*, 16 August 2007.

5   Barnett R. Rubin, 'Saving Afghanistan', *Foreign Affairs*, vol. 86, no. 1, January–February 2007, p. 78. Per-capita assistance to Afghanistan in 2002–03 was $67, significantly lower than the $256 provided to Timor Leste (1999–2001), the $249 provided to Bosnia-Herzegovina (1995–97) and the $219 provided to the West Bank and Gaza Strip (1994–2001) (Barnett R. Rubin et al., *Building a New Afghanistan: The Value of Success, the Cost of Failure* (New York: Center on International Cooperation, March 2004), p. 9). In terms of the provision of peacekeeping troops, a ratio of 1 soldier per 1,000 inhabitants has been deployed in Afghanistan, as compared to 20.5 in Kosovo, 19 in Bosnia, 10 in Sierra Leone and 3.5 in Haiti (Roland Paris, 'NATO's Choice in Afghanistan: Go Big or Go Home', *Policy Options*, December 2006–January 2007, p. 42).

6   Ahmed Rashid, 'Letter from Afghanistan: Are the Taliban Winning?', *Current History*, December 2006.

Chapter One

1   Antonio Giustozzi, *'Good State' vs. 'Bad Warlords'? A Critique of State-Building Strategies in Afghanistan*, Working Paper 51 (London: LSE Crisis States Programme, 2004).

2   Sarah Lister and Andrew Wilder, 'Strengthening Sub-National Administra-tion in Afghanistan: Technical Reform or State-Building', *Public Administration and Development*, no. 25, 2005, p. 41; Thomas Barfield, Neamat Nojumi and J. Alexander Thier, *The Clash of Two Goods: State and Non-State Dispute Resolution in Afghanistan*

(Washington DC: United States Institute of Peace, 2006), p. 13. A *shura* can be described as a village council, while a *jirga* is a traditional assembly.

3 The Bonn Agreement – officially the 'Agreement on Provisional Arrangements in Afghanistan Pending the Re-Establishment of Permanent Government Institutions' – was negotiated under the auspices of the United Nations. In it, the main representative factions and ethnic groups opposing the Taliban agreed on a framework within which the newly created Afghan Interim Authority (AIA) would rebuild state institutions.

4 Barnett R. Rubin, 'Peace-building and State-building in Afghanistan: Constructing Sovereignty for Whose Security?', *Third World Quarterly*, vol. 27, no. 1, pp. 175–85. Of the first group of 32 provincial governors appointed in 2002, 20 were militia commanders, warlords or strongmen. See Giustozzi, *'Good State' vs. 'Bad Warlords'?*.

5 *Ibid.*, p. 10.

6 Lister and Wilder, 'Strengthening Sub-National Administration in Afghanistan'.

7 Abdul Waheed Wafa, '32 Killed in Factional Fighting in Western Afghanistan', *New York Times*, 23 October 2006.

8 Interview with Western diplomat, Kabul, 19 June 2006.

9 Rachel Morajee, 'Karzai Faces Uphill Battle To Tame Afghan Parliament', Agence France-Presse, 14 September 2005; International Crisis Group (ICG), *Afghanistan's New Legislature: Making Democracy Work*, Asia Report 116 (Brussels: ICG, 2006), p. 4.

10 IRIN, 'Rights Body Warns of Warlords Success in Elections', 18 October 2005.

11 ICG, *Afghanistan's New Legislature*, p. 4.

12 It is important to approach public-opinion surveys undertaken in Afghanistan with a degree of caution, as the challenges of polling – insecurity, difficult topography and linguistic, ethnic and sectarian diversity – can make their results unreliable. For instance, some have argued that the HRRAC survey was skewed towards urban and educated Afghans and was not based on a representative sampling of the population as a whole. Comparable criticisms have been levelled at all the polls undertaken in Afghanistan since 2001.

13 IRIN, 'Rights Body Warns of Warlords Success in Elections'.

14 Interview with United Nations Assistance Mission for Afghanistan (UNAMA) official, Kabul, 12 November 2005.

15 Government of the Islamic Republic of Afghanistan, *Action Plan for Peace, Justice and Reconciliation in Afghanistan* (Kabul: GIRA, 2005); AIHRC website, http://www.aihrc.org.af/tj_actionplan_19_dec_05.htm; Andrew North, 'Afghans Adopt Justice Action Plan', BBC News, 12 December 2005, http://news.bbc.co.uk/1/hi/world/south_asia/4522624.stm.

Chapter Two

1 See Ahmed Rashid, *Taliban: The Story of the Afghan Warlords* (London: Pan Books, 2000).

2 Ali A. Jalali, 'The Legacy of War and the Challenge of Peace Building', in Robert I. Rotberg (ed.), *Building a New Afghanistan* (Washington DC: Brookings Institution Press and the World Peace Foundation, 2007), p. 4.

3 Interview with C. Christine Fair, senior research associate, South Asia and terrorism, Center for Conflict Analysis and Prevention, United States Institute of Peace, 27 December 2006.

4 Tablighi Jamaat (Proselytising Group) is the main worldwide Deobandi fundamentalist missionary movement.

5 The Deobandi line of Islam in South Asia originated in the north Indian city of Deoband in 1867. Although this movement

was Sufist in nature (and hence more tolerant), the Western Pakistan version of Deobandism had tremendous influence among Wahhabists and Salafists coming from Saudi Arabia and Egypt during the war against the Soviet Union. As a leading US military analyst has pointed out (interview, February 2007), one would find the Deoband madrassas in India of a more Sufist nature and truer to the roots of the movement.

6   The other components of the MMA are the Jamaat-i Islami (Party of Islam, JI), Tahrik-e-Islami (Movement of Islam), the Jamiat Ulema-e-Pakistan (Assembly of Pakistani Clerics, JUP) and the Jamiat-e-Ahle Hadith (Followers of the Prophet's Tradition).

7   The Darul Uloom Haqqania madrassa is 50km from Peshawar, in Akora Khattak. Its campus is spread across eight acres, and it hosts more than 3,000 students.

8   Rashid, *Taliban*, p. 91.

9   Rubin, 'Saving Afghanistan'.

10   General Mehmud Ahmed was instrumental in the October 1999 coup that brought Musharraf to power. His reward was promotion to the head of ISI.

11   Musharraf, quoted in 'Pakistani Intelligence Controversy', *Jane's Terrorism & Security Monitor*, 15 November 2006.

12   Seymour M. Hersh, 'The Getaway', *The New Yorker*, 28 January 2002, p. 36; and 'The Problem of Pakistan', *Jane's Intelligence Digest*, 15 March 2002.

13   Hassan Abbas, *Pakistan's Drift Into Extremism: Allah, the Army, and America's War On Terror* (Armonk, NY: M.E. Sharpe, 2004), pp. 201–16.

14   Amin Saikal, 'Securing Afghanistan's Border', *Survival*, vol. 48, no. 1, Spring 2006, p. 138. When asked who was behind the 11 September attacks, Gul replied: 'Mossad and its American associates'. Interview by Arnaud de Borchgrave with Hameed Gul, former ISI chief, United Press International, 26 September 2001.

15   Husain Haqqani, quoted in Alisa Tang, 'Afghan President Lashes Out at Pakistan', Associated Press, 14 December 2006.

16   'Pakistan Official Says India Training Baluchi Dissidents in Afghanistan', interview with Senator Mushahid Hussain Sayed, Pakistan Senate Foreign Relations Committee Chairman, Islamabad, 16 April 2006, in BBC Monitoring South Asia: 'India is gradually increasing the number of its paramilitary personnel in Afghanistan. From a few personnel, the strength of Indian troops has reached almost that of a company size force and even includes Black Cat Commandos.' See also Mariana Baabar, 'How India is Fomenting Trouble in Pakistan via Afghanistan', *The News*, 15 April 2006.

17   Barry Schweid, 'Pakistan Offers Afghanistan Border Fence', AP Diplomatic Writer, 12 September 2005.

18   *Landmine Monitor Report 2006*, http://www.icbl.org/lm/2006.

19   Carlotta Gall, 'Karzai Denounces Pakistan's Mining of Border', *New York Times*, 28 December 2006.

20   'US, Pakistani, Afghan Officials Hold First Three-Way Meeting', Agence France-Presse, 17 June 2003.

21   The intelligence centre has a staff of 24: 12 NATO officers, six officers from Pakistan and six from Afghanistan. 'Afghanistan and Pakistan Launch Intelligence-Sharing Centre', *Jane's Intelligence Digest*, 23 February 2007.

22   Michael Barry, *Le Royaume de l'Insolence – L'Afghanistan*, 1504–2001 (Paris : Flammarion, 2001).

23   Afzal Khan, 'Death of Tribal Leader Reveals Tribal Borderland may be Sanctuary for Taliban, Al-Qaeda Remnants', *Eurasia Daily Monitor*, 22 June 2004.

24   Of the Masood tribe who replaced Nek Mohammad, together with Haji Omar of the Wazir tribe.

25   Nirupama Subramanian, 'Backing Away from the Badlands?', *The Hindu*, 13 September 2006; and 'Historic Waziristan Peace Deal Signed', *The Nation*, 5 September 2006.

26   The text reads: 'All foreigners present in North Waziristan will leave Pakistan. For

those who could not leave due to some compulsion, it would be mandatory upon them that they respect the prevailing laws and this agreement and remain peaceful'.

27 'Pakistan's Dangerous Afghanistan Policy', *Jane's Intelligence Digest*, 3 November 2006.

28 '2.3 Tons Hashish, Morphine Seized', *Dawn*, 9 December 2002; 'Arms Cache Seized', *The Daily Times*, 13 August 2004; and 'Taliban Insurgency Shows Signs of Enduring Strength', *Jane's Intelligence Review*, 1 October 2006.

29 Dexter Filkins, 'US Might Pursue Qaeda and Taliban to Pakistan Lairs', *New York Times*, 21 March 2002.

30 Wolf Blitzer, The Situation Room, CNN, 20 September 2006.

31 'Bin Laden Search Hampered by Musharraf's Dilemma', *Jane's Foreign Report*, 7 July 2005.

32 'US Ties with Pakistan Under Strain', *Jane's Intelligence Digest*, 23 June 2006.

33 Bob Woodward, 'Secret CIA Units Playing a Central Combat Role', *Washington Post*, 18 November 2001.

34 'Internecine Struggles among Kashmiri Militants', *Jane's Islamic Affairs Analyst*, 1 July 2000.

35 National Commission on Terrorist Attacks upon the United States, *The 9/11 Commission Report*, 22 July 2004, p. 123 and p. 483, n. 74.

36 'Designation of Lashkar I Jhangvi as a Foreign Terrorist Organization', US State Department, Washington DC, 30 January 2003.

37 'Lashkar-e-Taiba Spreads Its Tentacles', *Jane's Terrorism & Security Monitor*, 1 September 2004.

38 'The Kashmir Connection', *Jane's Terrorism & Security Monitor*, 13 September 2006.

39 ICG, *Pakistan's Tribal Areas: Appeasing the Militants*, ICG Asia Report 125 (Brussels: ICG, 11 December 2006).

40 US Major-General Benjamin Freakley, in Pamela Constable, 'Dozens Are Killed in Afghanistan Fighting', *Washington Post*, 23 May 2006; Peter Bergen, 'The Taliban, Regrouped and Rearmed', 10 September 2006, http://www.peterbergen.com/bergen/articles/details.aspx?id=277; Barnett Rubin, Prepared Testimony for the House Committee on International Relations, CFR, 20 September 2006, and General James Jones Jr, Supreme Allied Commander (SACEUR) US European Command, NATO, in US Senator Richard Lugar, Hearing on Afghanistan Command Transition to the International Security Assistance Force, US Senate Committee on Foreign Relations Hearing, 21 September 2006.

41 Omid Marzban and Mullah Dadullah, 'The Military Mastermind of the Taliban Insurgency', *Terrorism Focus*, vol. 3, no. 11, 21 March 2006.

42 'Increasing Afghan IED Threat Gives Forces Cause for Concern', *Jane's Intelligence Review*, 1 August 2006; and Anthony H. Cordesman, 'Winning Afghanistan: Facing the Rising Threat', Center for Strategic and International Studies, 13 December 2006.

43 'US Genl: Top Afghan Insurgent Leader Operating in Pakistan', Dow Jones International News, 13 January 2007.

44 'The Other Taliban; Pakistan', *The Economist*, 18 March 2006.

45 Ahmed Rashid, cited in 'US: Airstrike Kills Taliban Commander', Associated Press, 24 December 2006.

46 'Bin Laden's "Close Associate" Killed in Southern Afghanistan', Agence France-Presse, 23 December 2006.

47 Rahimullah Yusufzai, 'Taleban's Most Feared Commander', BBC News, 13 May 2007, http://news.bbc.co.uk/2/hi/south_asia/4998836.stm.

48 Statement of Peter Bergen, Senior Fellow, New America Foundation, Committee on House Foreign Affairs, 15 February 2007: 'Dadullah put Taliban forces at some 12,000 fighters, larger than a US military official's estimate to me of between 7,000 to 10,000, but a number that could have some validity given the numerous part-time Taliban farmer/fighters'.

49 'Factbox–Military Deaths in Afghanistan', Reuters, 28 December 2006.

50 Jean-Luc Marret, *The Evolution of Jihadi Profiles*, Working Paper, Center for Transatlantic Relations, Johns Hopkins University, Fondation pour la Recherche Stratégique, 11 December 2006.

51 David Montero, 'Elders Losing to Extremists in Pakistan', *Christian Science Monitor*, 8 June 2006; and Declan Walsh, 'New Frontline in the War on Terror: Waziristan', *The Guardian*, 4 May 2006.

52 In December 2006, a nine-page stapled pamphlet printed by the Taliban and signed by Mullah Omar was distributed in Afghanistan. The *Layeha* (*Book of Rules*) lays down 29 rules for Taliban recruits. Rules of engagement are described for 'soft targets', especially government schools, stating that Taliban recruits must first warn teachers to stop teaching, and only beat them up if they refuse to comply; the unit commander is to kill them if they are 'found to be teaching against Islam'. The book also tells Taliban soldiers not to loot indiscriminately, and orders them not to kill Afghans working with 'infidels' if they are willing to join the movement. Sami Yousafzai and Ron Moreau, 'By the Book: Taliban Fighters Play By Their Own Rules', *Newsweek*, 3 December 2006.

53 'Gates Says Cross-Border Attacks in Afghanistan a "Problem"', Agence France-Presse, 16 January 2007.

54 Declan Walsh, 'Eyewitness: Spin Boldak, Afghanistan: Afghans Struggle To Police Gateway to Terror', *The Guardian*, 22 June 2006.

55 'Increasing Afghan IED Threat Gives Forces Cause for Concern', *Jane's Intelligence Review*, 1 August 2006.

56 'US Commander Wants More Troops Against Taliban Surge', Agence France-Presse, 16 January 2007.

57 See http://www.youtube.com/watch?v=c9bdo91qFo8.

58 The website was until recently at http://www.alemarah.org.

59 Michael Smith, 'SBS Behind Taliban Leader's Death', *Sunday Times*, 27 May 2007.

60 Barnett Rubin, interview transcript, Frontline, 3 October 2006, http://www.pbs.org/wgbh/pages/frontline/taliban/interviews/rubin.html.

61 Evan F. Kohlmann, 'The Real Online Terrorist Threat', *Foreign Affairs*, vol. 85, no. 5, September–October 2006.

62 Interview with Dr Mathieu Guidere, Centre de Recherche des Ecoles de Coëtquidan (CREC), Saint-Cyr Military Academy, France, April 2006.

63 *Psychological Operations: An Overview*, US Department of Defense, Doctrine for Joint Psychological Operations, 5 September 2003, chapter 1.

64 Declan Walsh, 'Afghan Schools Under Siege as Taliban Maintain Grip', *Boston Globe*, 16 March 2006; and *Lessons in Terror: Attacks on Education in Afghanistan*, Human Rights Watch, vol. 18, no. 6 (C), July 2006.

65 The other main Pashtun tribal group is the Durrani.

66 The 'Peshawar 7': Hezb-i Islami (Gulbuddin Hekmatyar and Yunus Khales branches); Jamaat-e-Islami (Islamic Society) of Burhanuddin Rabbani; Itehad Islami (Islamic Unity) of Abdul Rasul Sayyaf; Mahaz-i-Milli Islam (National Islamic Front of Afghanistan) of Pir Sayed Ahmad Gilani; Jabha-i-Nijat-Milli (Afghan National Liberation Front) of Sibgratullah Mojaddedi; and Harakat-i-Inqilab-i-Islami (Islamic Revolutionary Forces) of Mohammad Nabi Mohammadi.

67 Al-Jazeera, 6 May 2006.

68 Omid Marzban, 'Gulbuddin Hekmatyar: From Holy Warrior to Wanted Terrorist', *Terrorism Monitor*, vol. 4, no. 18, 21 September 2006.

69 'Fourth Generation Warfare and the International Jihad', *Jane's Intelligence Review*, 1 October 2006.

70 Gary Bernsten and Ralph Pezzullo, *Jawbreaker: The Attack on Bin Laden and Al Qaeda: A Personal Account by the CIA's Key Field Commander* (New York: Three Rivers Press, 2005), p. 308.

71 Philip G. Smucker, *Al Qaeda's Great Escape: The Military and the Media on Terror's Trail* (Dulles, VA: Potomac Books, April 2005).

72 Victor Korgun, 'Afghanistan's Resurgent Taliban', *Terrorism Monitor*, vol. 1, no. 4, October 2003.

73 Arnaud de Borchgrave, 'A Ride on the Wild Side', *Washington Times*, 25 September 2005.

74 Ahmed Rashid, 'Don't Think Al-Qaeda is on the Back Foot, it will be on the March in 2007', *Sunday Telegraph*, 31 December 2006.

75 Hassan Abbas, 'The Black-Turbaned Brigade: The Rise of TNSM in Pakistan', *Terrorism Monitor*, vol. 4, no. 23, 30 November 2006.

76 In 2005, Karzai discreetly gave his backing to Sayyaf over Yunus Qanuni, a leading Panjshiri figure, to be speaker of parliament. 'A Place for Warlords To Meet; Afghanistan', *The Economist*, 7 January 2006.

77 *Have Hekmatyar's Radicals Reformed?*, Institute for War and Peace Reporting, ARR no. 210, 6 April 2006.

78 For the ethnic breakdown of Afghanistan, see the CIA *World Factbook*, which estimates Pashtun 42%, Tajik 27%, Hazara 9%, Uzbek 9%, Aimak 4%, Turkmen 3%, Baloch 2% and other groups 4%, https://www.cia.gov/cia/publications/factbook/print/af.html.

79 Kenneth Katzman, *Iran: US Concerns and Policy Responses*, CRS Report for Congress, 11 February 2005.

80 'Iran Arming Taliban, US Claims', CNN.com, 13 June 2007, http://www.cnn.com/2007/WORLD/asiapcf/06/13/iran.taliban/index.html.

81 'Gates: US Has Evidence of Iran Helping Insurgents', CNN.com, 9 February 2007, http://www.cnn.com/2007/POLITICS/02/09/gates.iraq.iran.ap/index.html; and Michael R. Gordon, 'US Says Iranian Arms Seized in Afghanistan', *New York Times*, 18 April 2007.

82 'Iraq-Style Bomb Found In Afghanistan', CBS News, 2 June 2007, http://www.cbsnews.com/stories/2007/06/02/world/main2878128.shtml?source=RSS&attr=_2878128.

Chapter Three

1 All the opium-related figures used here, unless stated otherwise, are from Doris Buddenberg and William A. Byrd (eds), *Afghanistan's Drug Industry: Structure, Functioning, Dynamics, and Implications for Counter-Narcotics Policy* (Kabul: United Nations Office on Drugs and Crime (UNODC) and the World Bank, November 2006), and from the 2007 Annual Opium Poppy Survey in Afghanistan, http://www.unodc.org/pdf/research/AFG07_ExSum_web.pdf.

2 Pierre-Arnaud Chouvy, 'Afghanistan's Opium Production in Perspective', *China and Eurasia Forum Quarterly: Narcotics*, vol. 4, no. 1, February 2006.

3 Keeping in mind that Afghanistan then had a surplus opium stockpile of 2,900 tonnes.

4 Chouvy, 'Afghanistan's Opium Production', p. 124; and Pierre-Arnaud Chouvy, 'Les Territoires de l'Opium', *Olizane*, 2002, pp. 64–7.

5 'Iran's Drug Problem', *Jane's Intelligence Review*, 2 February 2007.

6 David Mansfield, *Exploring the 'Shades of Grey': An Assessment of the Factors Influencing Decisions to Cultivate Opium Poppy in 2005/06*, Report for the Afghan Drugs Inter Departmental Unit of the UK government, March 2005.

7 Jonathan Goodhand, 'Frontiers and Wars: A Study of the Opium Economy in Afghanistan', *Journal of Agrarian Change*, vol. 5, no. 2, April 2005, p. 191.

8 George Packer, 'Knowing the Enemy: A Reporter at Large', *The New Yorker*, 18 December 2006.

9 Carlotta Gall, 'Opium Harvest at Record Level in Afghanistan', *New York Times*, 3 September 2006.

10 Alain Labrousse, *Opium de Guerre, Opium de Paix* (Paris: Mille et Une Nuits Editions, 2005), pp. 117–20.

11 Interviews with General Daud, Deputy Interior Minister for Counter Narcotics, and international counter-narcotics officials, Kabul, May 2006.

12 Interview with UNODC official, Kabul, May 2006.

13 Interview with UK government security adviser, Kabul, May 2006.

14 A more realistic figure is in the range of 3–3.5 million: 'Iran's Drug Problem'.

15 Interview, Kabul, May 2006.

16 By weight of opiates seized. Buddenberg and Byrd (eds), *Afghanistan's Drug Industry*.

17 Rubin, 'Saving Afghanistan'.

18 'The Changing Structure of the Afghan Opium Trade', *Jane's Intelligence Review*, 9 September 2006.

19 Gall, 'Opium Harvest at Record Level'.

20 Barnett Rubin, *The Political Economy of War and Peace in Afghanistan*, 1999, http://www.eurasianet.org/resource/regional/rubin_on_afgistan.html.

21 Joanna Wright, 'Afghanistan's Opiate Economy and Terrorist Financing', *Jane's Intelligence Review*, 1 March 2006.

22 Interview with former Interior Minister Ali Jalali, November 2006.

23 Alexandre Peyrille, 'Afghanistan Destroys 100 Tons of Opium', Agence France-Presse, 20 April 2002. Ghani told reporters: 'In Helmand and Nangahar provinces, 2,939,000 dollars have been paid out in total and 2,060 hectares (5,088 acres) have been destroyed … We are fully confident that local governors are on board with this programme and will support us'.

24 'After Victory, Defeat – Afghanistan', *The Economist*, 16 July 2005.

25 Victoria Burnett and Mark Huband, 'UK Trains Afghans in Anti-Drugs Drive', *Financial Times*, 10 January 2004.

26 Michael A. Braun, Chief of Operations, Drug Enforcement Administration, Testimony Before the Committee on International Relations, US House of Representatives, 17 March 2005.

27 National Drug Control Strategy, Islamic Republic of Afghanistan, Ministry of Counter Narcotics, http://www.mcn.gov.af.

28 Anne W. Patterson, US Assistant Secretary for International Narcotics and Law Enforcement Affairs, Department of State, Afghanistan Interdiction/Eradication of Illegal Narcotics and US Lead Rebuilding Programs, Testimony Before the House Committee on Appropriations Subcommittee on Foreign Operations, Export Financing and Related Programs, Washington DC, 12 September 2006, http://www.state.gov/p/inl/rls/rm/72241.htm.

29 House Appropriations Foreign Operations, Export Financing and Related Programs Subcommittee Hearing on Afghanistan Interdiction, Eradication of Illegal Narcotics and Rebuilding Programs, 12 September 2006. In May 2006, only four judges were trained to tackle counter-narcotics issues for the whole country, according to a high-ranking UN official interviewed in Kabul.

30 Antonio Maria Costa, 'Foreword', in *2007 Annual Opium Poppy Survey in Afghanistan, Executive Summary*.

31 Jean MacKenzie, Wahidullah Amani and Sayed Yaqub Ibrahimi, 'Why Afghanistan Is Losing the War on Drugs', *San Diego Union-Tribune*, 17 December 2006.

32 'Afghan Drug Kingpin Detained in US', Agence France-Presse, 25 April 2005.

33 'US Announces Historic Extradition of Taliban-Linked Afghan Narco-Terrorist to New York', US Newswire, 24 October 2005.

34 UNODC, *The Opium Situation in Afghanistan*, 29 August 2005.

35 Jason Straziuso, 'US Anti-Drug Chief: Afghan Poppies To Be Sprayed with Herbicide', Associated Press, 2 December 2006.

36 Pierre-Arnaud Chouvy, 'Afghan Opium: License to Kill', *Asia Times*, 1 February 2006.

37 The International Narcotics Control Board (INCB) 2004 report points out that: 'The

Board notes with appreciation that most Governments of producing countries have adhered to its recommendations and taken action to reduce the production of opiate raw materials, those rich in morphine and those rich in thebaine, to reflect the global demand for those raw materials. For both types of raw materials, production had, until recently, been increasing at levels well in excess of global demand.' See http://www.incb.org.

38 'Afghan Ministry Welcomes Senate's Condemnation of Senlis Council', BBC Monitoring South Asia, 28 May 2006.

39 See 'Afghan Paper Asks Senlis Council To Clarify Questions', BBC Monitoring South Asia, 6 September 2006.

Chapter Four

1 Statement by General Tommy R. Franks, Commander in Chief, US Central Command, Senate Armed Services Committee, 7 February 2002.

2 While OEF usually refers to the war in Afghanistan, two other subordinate OEF operations are being conducted in parallel, OEF–Philippines and OEF–Horn of Africa, both focusing on monitoring and disrupting transnational terrorists operating in their regions.

3 Lawrence Freedman, *The Transformation of Strategic Affairs*, Adelphi Paper 379 (Milton Park, Routledge for the IISS, April 2006), p. 61.

4 Bernsten and Pezzullo, *Jawbreaker*, p. 314.

5 *Ibid*.

6 Mark Hewish, 'Underground Attack Initiatives Expand', *Jane's International Defense Review*, 1 November 2002.

7 Military Technical Agreement Between the International Security Assistance Force (ISAF) and the Interim Administration of Afghanistan ('Interim Administration'), Article IV: Deployment of the ISAF, Chapter 3.

8 The British public did not have a clear sense of the mission either. An ICM poll for the BBC found that nearly half (46%) believed that the purpose of UK involvement in Afghanistan was to stop the flow of drugs. Raymond Whitaker, 'Afghanistan', *The Independent*, 5 November 2006.

9 France had around 200 special forces troops from the Special Operations Command based in Spin Boldak and Jalalabad, under US command. At the end of 2006, then French Minister of Defence Michelle Alliot-Marie announced that they were being withdrawn from Afghanistan.

10 The Ink Spot strategy was first used by the British against the communist insurgency in Malaya in the 1950s. It was invented by Sir Gerald Templer, the British High Commissioner in Malaya between 1952 and 1954. Templer also coined the phrase 'winning hearts and minds'.

11 Lieutenant-General Karl Eikenberry, US Commander, Combined Forces Command–Afghanistan (CFC-A), Defense Department News Briefing, 21 September 2006.

12 Michael Smith, 'British Troops in Secret Truce with the Taliban', *Sunday Times*, 1 October 2006.

13 Kim Sengupta, 'NATO Troops Kill Up To 80 Militants in Helmand', *The Independent*, 5 December 2006.

14 Anthony H. Cordesman, *Winning Afghanistan: Facing the Rising Threat* (Washington DC: Center for Strategic and International Studies, 5 December 2006).

15 See *NATO in Afghanistan Factsheet*, http://www.nato.int/issues/afghanistan/040628-factsheet.htm.

16 Robert M. Perito, *The US Experience with Provincial Reconstruction Teams in Afghanistan, Lessons Identified* (Washington DC: US Institute of Peace, October 2005).

17 David W. Barno, 'Afghanistan: The Security Outlook', address delivered at the Center for Security and International Studies (CSIS), Washington DC, 14 May 2004, p. 10, available at: http://www.csis.org/isp/pcr/040514_barno.pdf.

18 Michael J. Dziedzic and Colonel Michael K. Seidl, *Provincial Reconstruction Teams and Military Relations with International and Nongovernmental Organizations in Afghanistan*, United States Institute of Peace Special Report 147 (Washington DC: USIP, September 2005); and Mark Sedra, *Civil–Military Relations in Afghanistan: The Provincial Reconstruction Team Debate*, available at: http://asiapacificresearch.ca/caprn/afghan_project/m_sedra.pdf.

19 Mark M. Lowenthal, *Intelligence: From Secret to Policy* (Washington DC: CQ Press, 2006), pp. 27 and 86.

20 Interviews with US special forces field officers, Kabul, May 2006, and Boston, MA, November 2006.

Chapter Five

1 Opening Address by President Hamid Karzai to the National Symposium on Security Sector Reform, 30 July 2003.

2 Mark Sedra, 'Security Sector Reform in Afghanistan: The Slide Toward Expediency', *International Peacekeeping*, vol. 13, no. 1, March 2006.

3 See Emma Sky, 'The Lead Nation Approach: The Case of Afghanistan', *RUSI Journal*, December 2006.

4 The framework had been introduced at the January 2002 Tokyo donor conference, but took form at Geneva.

5 US Government Accountability Office (GAO), *Afghanistan Security: Efforts To Establish Army and Police Have Made Progress, But Future Plans Need To Be Better Defined* (Washington DC: GAO, June 2005), p. 9.

6 Petersberg Declaration, *Rebuilding Afghanistan: Peace and Stability*, 2 December 2002.

7 United Nations Secretary-General, *The Situation in Afghanistan and Its Implications for International Peace and Security*, A/56/875-S/2002/878 (New York: United Nations, March 2002), p. 10.

8 Ministry of Defence of Afghanistan, *National Military Strategy* (Kabul: Ministry of Defence of Afghanistan, 2004), p. 10.

9 In July 2005, the Office of Military Cooperation–Afghanistan (OMC-A) was renamed the Office of Security Cooperation–Afghanistan (OSC-A), after it assumed responsibility for supporting the police as well as the Afghan military. Its name was changed again in May 2006, to the Combined Security Transition Command–Afghanistan (CSTC-A).

10 Combined Security Transition Command–Afghanistan (CSCT-A), *Fact Sheet: Afghan National Army (ANA) Organization, Training and Operations*, April 2006, http://oneteam.centcom.mil/default.aspx. The plan was to move to a six-*kandak* model in December 2006.

11 GAO, *Afghanistan Security*, pp. 17–18

12 Interview with CSCT-A officials, Kabul, 24 June 2006.

13 Interview with Lieutenant-General Karl W. Eikenberry, Kabul, 19 June 2006.

14 Interview with CSCT-A officials, Kabul, 24 June 2006.

15 *Ibid.*

16 Jim Garamone, 'Pace Pleased with Progress at Afghan Training Center', *American Forces Press Service*, 23 April 2007, http://www.defenselink.mil/news/newsarticle.aspx?id=32901.

17 *The Afghanistan Compact: Building on Success*, February 2006, Annex 1.

18 US Department of Defense, News Briefing with Lieutenant-General Karl W. Eikenberry and Minister of Defence

Abdul Rahim Wardak in the Pentagon, transcript, 21 November 2006.

[19] Helene Cooper and David S. Cloud, 'Bush To Seek More Aid for Afghanistan as Taliban Regroups', *New York Times*, 26 January 2007.

[20] Barnett R. Rubin, *Afghanistan's Uncertain Transition From Turmoil to Normalcy* (Washington DC: Council on Foreign Relations, 2006), pp. 21–2.

[21] World Bank, *Afghanistan: Managing Public Finances for Development – Improving Public Finance Management in the Security Sector* (Washington DC: World Bank, 2005), pp. 42–3.

[22] Interview with CSTC-A officials, Kabul, 24 June 2006.

[23] 'Defence Minister Says Afghan Army Must Be 5 Times Larger', Associated Press, 12 July 2006.

[24] *Ibid.*

[25] Interview with senior Ministry of Counter-Narcotics official, Kabul, 18 June 2006; interview with senior Interior Ministry official, 23 June 2006.

[26] CSTC-A, *Factsheet*.

[27] Islamic Republic of Afghanistan, *Afghanistan National Development Strategy (ANDS) Sector Summary Report* (Kabul: Islamic Republic of Afghanistan, 2006).

[28] David Zucchino, 'It's Starting To Look a Lot Like an Army', *Los Angeles Times*, 22 August 2006.

[29] Interview with CSTC-A officials, Kabul, 24 June 2006.

[30] Telephone interview, NATO official, 23 October 2006.

[31] As of June 2007, the following nations had contributed full OMLTs/ETTs: Canada, Croatia, France, Germany, Italy, the Netherlands, Poland, Spain, the UK and the US.

[32] Anthony H. Cordesman, *Winning in Afghanistan: Afghan Force Development* (Washington DC: CSIS, 2006).

[33] Major Rick Peat and Lieutenant-Colonel Frederick Rice, 'Afghan Military Academy Opens Gates to Future Leaders', American Forces Press Service, 28 March 2005.

[34] Interview with CSTC-A officials, Kabul, 24 June 2006.

[35] 'Afghanistan Celebrates Opening of Command and General Staff College', American Forces Press Service, 30 October 2006.

[36] Ministry of Defence of Afghanistan, *Afghan National Army: The Future of a Nation* (Kabul: Ministry of Defence of Afghanistan, 2006).

[37] *Ibid.*

[38] Interview with Military Professional Resources Incorporated (MPRI) official, Kabul, 21 June 2006. There are 2–3 MTTs in the field at any one time; they spend between two weeks and a month providing training down to the battalion level.

[39] Jim Garamone, 'Pace Pleased with Progress at Afghan Training Center'.

[40] Antonio Giustozzi and Mark Sedra, *Securing Afghanistan's Future: Accomplishments and the Strategic Pathway Forward – Afghan National Army Technical Annex* (Kabul: Islamic Transitional State of Afghanistan, 2004).

[41] Elaine Shannon, 'Can More Aid Save Afghanistan?', *Time*, 26 January 2007.

[42] Giustozzi and Sedra, *Securing Afghanistan's Future*.

[43] MPRI has been contracted to develop the personnel management, payroll and leave system. Interview with MPRI official, Kabul, 21 June 2006.

[44] Antonio Giustozzi, 'Military Reform in Afghanistan', in Mark Sedra (ed.), *Confronting Afghanistan's Security Dilemma: Reforming the Security Sector*, Brief 28 (Bonn: Bonn International Center for Conversion, 2003).

[45] Anja Manuel and P.W. Singer, 'A New Model Afghan Army', *Foreign Affairs*, vol. 8, no. 4, July–August 2002, p. 57.

[46] See Chapter 2, note 78.

[47] Such allegations are difficult to verify because the US and the Afghan government have refused to reveal a precise ethnic breakdown of the ANA.

[48] Interview with Ustad Mohammed Mohaqqeq, Kabul, 16 June 2006; interview

with Vice-President Abdul Karim Khalili, Kabul, 18 June 2006.

49 Interview with MPRI official, Kabul, 21 June 2006.

50 Ibid.

51 Seema Patel, Breaking Point: Measuring Progress in Afghanistan (Washington DC: Center for Security and International Studies, 2007), p. 38.

52 Personal communication with Western donor official, 31 August 2007.

53 David Zucchino, 'Afghan Army Could Help Unify a Nation', Los Angeles Times, 13 November 2006.

54 Ministry of Defence of Afghanistan, Afghan National Army.

55 Ibid.

56 Zucchino, 'Afghan Army Could Help Unify a Nation'.

57 US Department of Defense, News Briefing with Major-General Robert Durbin and Deputy Minister Abdul Hadir Khalid from in the Pentagon, transcript, 9 January 2007.

58 Ibid.

59 Interview with Deputy Minister of Defence Yusuf Nuristani, Kabul, 20 June 2006.

60 GAO, Afghanistan Security, p. 16.

61 Trini Tran, 'US Giving Afghans $2B Worth of Weaponry', Associated Press, 3 July 2006. This is in addition to the roughly $2bn already expended on ANA equipment and infrastructure up to 2006.

62 Zucchino, 'Afghan Army Could Help Unify a Nation'.

63 United Nations Secretary-General, The Situation in Afghanistan and Its Implications for International Peace and Security, A/59/744-S/2005/183 (New York: United Nations, March 2005), p. 5.

64 Interview with MPRI official, Kabul, 21 June 2006.

65 Ibid.

66 Ibid; interview with Western adviser to the Ministry of Defence, Kabul, 14 November 2005.

67 Interview with CSTC-A official, Kabul, 21 June 2006.

68 Ibid.

69 Interview with Western adviser to the Ministry of Defence, Kabul, 14 November 2005.

70 Carlotta Gall, 'Anti-US Rioting Erupts in Kabul; At Least 14 Dead', New York Times, 30 May 2006.

71 Carlotta Gall, 'Afghans Raise Toll of Dead from May Riots in Kabul to 17', New York Times, 8 June 2006.

72 Interview with CARE Afghanistan Country Director Paul Barker, Kabul, 24 June 2006. The police reportedly donned salwar kameez in an attempt to conceal their uniforms. Others took off their uniforms altogether in favour of civilian clothing.

73 Interview with NGO representative, Kabul, 25 June 2006.

74 Tonita Murray, 'Police-Building in Afghanistan: A Case Study of Civil Security Building', International Peacekeeping, vol. 14, no. 1, January 2007, pp. 122–3.

75 Interview with senior Interior Ministry official, Kabul, 23 June 2006; Scott Baldauf, 'Inside the Afghan Drug Trade', Christian Science Monitor, 13 June 2006.

76 Interview with senior Interior Ministry official, Kabul, 23 June 2006; interview with international police adviser, Kabul, 20 June 2006.

77 Rubin, 'Saving Afghanistan', p. 67.

78 Institute for War and Peace Reporting, Afghan Press Monitor, no. 51, 25 November 2004.

79 German Federal Foreign Office and Federal Ministry of Interior, Assistance for Rebuilding the Police Force in Afghanistan (Berlin: Federal Foreign Ministry and Federal Ministry of Interior, 2005), p. 8.

80 Inspectors General of the US Department of State and the US Department of Defense, Interagency Assessment of Afghanistan Police Training and Readiness (Washington DC: Department of State and Department of Defense, November 2006), p. 5. This force figure could be broken down as follows: 44,300 regular police, 12,000 border police, 3,400 highway police and 2,300 counter-narcotics police.

However, this blueprint was superseded by amendments to the size and structure of the ANP in 2006, which saw the force target expanded to 82,000, the creation of a standby police unit and the disbanding of the highway police.

81 Interview with UNAMA official, Kabul, 13 June 2006.

82 ICG, *Reforming Afghanistan's Police* (Brussels: ICG, 2007), p. 10.

83 German Embassy in Washington, *Secure and Democratic Future for Afghanistan: Germany's Commitment*, 2006, http://www.germany.info/relaunch/info/archives/background/Afghanistan_factsheet.pdf; German Federal Foreign Office and Federal Ministry of Interior, *Assistance for Rebuilding the Police Force in Afghanistan*, p. 9; personal communication with Afghan Research and Evaluation Unit (AREU) researcher, 10 February 2007.

84 Interview with Norwegian police project official, Kabul, 3 May 2005.

85 German Federal Foreign Office and Federal Ministry of Interior, *Assistance For Rebuilding the Police Force in Afghanistan*, p. 11. Of these, 57 graduates were women.

86 Mark Sedra, *Challenging the Warlord Culture: Security Sector Reform in Afghanistan*, Paper 25 (Bonn: Bonn International Center for Conversion, 2002).

87 The topics covered by the curriculum included crime investigation, operational police skills and human rights. Due to a lack of weapons and ammunition, trainees did not receive firearms training until 2006. Thirty DynCorp advisers were originally dispatched across the country to conduct the training. GAO, *Afghanistan Security*, p. 23.

88 *Ibid.*, p. 20; Pam O'Toole, 'Afghan Police "Under-equipped"', BBC News Online, 13 July 2007, http://news.bbc.co.uk/go/pr/fr/-/1/hi/world/south_asia/6897051.stm.

89 GAO, *Afghanistan Security*, p. 20.

90 Inspectors General of the US Department of State and the US Department of Defense, *Interagency Assessment of Afghanistan Police Training and Readiness*, p. 15.

91 *Ibid.*, p. 16.

92 *Ibid.*, p. 22.

93 The police have borne the brunt of casualties in the ongoing insurgency with the Taliban. Between May 2006 and May 2007, 406 ANP were killed, more than twice the number of fatalities in the ANA over the same period (ICG, *Reforming Afghanistan's Police*, p. 14).

94 Inspectors General of the US Department of State and the US Department of Defense, *Interagency Assessment of Afghanistan Police Training and Readiness*, p. 22.

95 O'Toole, 'Afghan Police "Under-equipped"'.

96 Equipment donations from the international community totalled $92.5m from FY2002 to 2006; Inspectors-General of the US Department of State and the US Department of Defense, *Interagency Assessment of Afghanistan Police Training and Readiness*, p. 44.

97 *Ibid.*

98 *Ibid.*, p. 20.

99 Interview with CSTC-A officials, Kabul, 24 June 2006.

100 Inspectors-General of the US Department of State and the US Department of Defense, *Interagency Assessment of Afghanistan Police Training and Readiness*, pp. 20–21.

101 Interview with senior Interior Ministry official, Kabul, 23 June 2006; Rubin, 'Saving Afghanistan', p. 69.

102 Interview with senior ANBP official, Kabul, 30 April 2005; ICG, *Afghanistan: Getting Disarmament Back on Track* (Brussels: ICG, 2005), p. 7.

103 ICG, *Afghanistan: Getting Disarmament Back on Track*, p. 7.

104 Interview with senior ANP official, Kabul, 19 June 2006.

105 *Ibid.*

106 ICG, *Reforming Afghanistan's Police*, p. 7. Some mentors will also come from the military and MPRI.

107 Inspectors-General of the US Department of State and the US Department of Defense, *Interagency Assessment of*

Afghanistan Police Training and Readiness, p. 25.

108 Ahto Lobjakas, 'Afghanistan: EU Aid Targets Justice System', Radio Free Europe/Radio Liberty, 12 February 2007.

109 Telephone interview with Professor Ali A. Jalali, 16 November 2006.

110 Interview with GPPO official, Kabul, 6 November 2005.

111 Interview with senior Interior Ministry official, Kabul, 23 June 2006; Baldauf, 'Inside the Afghan Drug Trade'.

112 Interview with GPPO official, Kabul, 6 November 2005.

113 The *tashkil* is an organisational document which dictates force structure, personnel end-strength, command relationships and unit/staff functions.

114 Rubin, 'Saving Afghanistan'; telephone interview with Ali A. Jalali, 16 November 2006.

115 Interview with EC official, Kabul, 22 June 2006.

116 Andrew Wilder, *Cops or Robbers: The Struggle to Reform the Afghan National Police* (Kabul: Afghan Research and Evaluation Unit, July 2007), p. 38. To facilitate the efficient delivery of salaries to the ANP, the US has established a programme to build the capacity of the Ministry of Interior Finance Department, notably in developing the Planning, Programming and Budgeting and Pay Master system (Inspectors General of the US Department of State and the US Department of Defense, *Interagency Assessment of Afghanistan Police Training and Readiness*, p. 28).

117 Interview with EC official, Kabul, 22 June 2006.

118 Wilder, *Cops or Robbers*, p. 24.

119 World Bank, *Afghanistan: Managing Public Finances for Development*, p. 46; Islamic Republic of Afghanistan, *Implementation of the Afghanistan Compact: Bi-Annual JCMB Report* (Kabul: Islamic Republic of Afghanistan, November 2006), p. 6.

120 GAO, *Afghanistan Security*, p. 26.

121 Interview with GPPO official, Kabul, 6 November 2005.

122 *Ibid*.

123 ICG, *Reforming Afghanistan's Police*, pp. 8–9; Wilder, *Cops or Robbers*, pp. 19–20.

124 ICG, *Reforming Afghanistan's Police*, p. 8.

125 Interview with GPPO official, Kabul, 14 June 2006.

126 Inspectors General of the US Department of State and the US Department of Defense, *Interagency Assessment of Afghanistan Police Training and Readiness*, p. 18.

127 Interview with GPPO official, Kabul, 14 June 2006.

128 Wilder, *Cops or Robbers*, pp. 27–8.

129 *Ibid*; ICG, *Reforming Afghanistan's Police*, p. 9.

130 Captain Dave Huxsoll, 'Afghan Interior Ministry Reforms Rank, Pay Structures', DefendAmerica, 4 November 2005, http://www.defendamerica.mil.

131 Inspectors-General of the US Department of State and the US Department of Defense, *Interagency Assessment of Afghanistan Police Training and Readiness*, p. 27.

132 Huxsoll, 'Afghan Interior Ministry Reforms Rank, Pay Structures'.

133 Interview with GPPO official, Kabul, 14 June 2006. One of the 14 candidates did not sit the written test, while the remaining 13 were not subjected to the file review process.

134 Declan Walsh, 'UN Report Sheds Light on Afghans' Darkest Deeds', *San Francisco Chronicle*, 17 June 2006.

135 Interview with CSTC-A officials, Kabul, 24 June 2006.

136 UNAMA, Press Briefing Transcript, 17 January 2007, www.unama-afg.org.

137 Wilder, *Cops or Robbers*, pp. 41–2.

138 *Ibid*.

139 *Ibid*.

140 Afghanistan Ministry of Interior, *Afghan National Police: In Service for the People* (Kabul: Afghanistan Ministry of Interior and CSTC-A, 2006); interview with GPPO official, Kabul, 14 June 2006.

141 Interview with international police adviser, Kabul, 20 June 2006. The system is intended to be funded by LOTFA.

142 Islamic Republic of Afghanistan, *Implementation of the Afghanistan Compact*.

143 Inspectors-General of the US Department of State and the US Department of Defense, *Interagency Assessment of Afghanistan Police Training and Readiness*, p. 29. It is envisioned that the temporary police will be integrated into the regular ANP after one year of service.

144 Mark Sedra, *Securing Afghanistan's Future: Accomplishments and Strategic Pathway Forward – National Police and Law Enforcement Technical Annex* (Kabul: Islamic Transitional State of Afghanistan, 2004).

145 Interview with MPRI official, Kabul, 21 June 2006.

146 Inspectors-General of the US Department of State and the US Department of Defense, *Interagency Assessment of Afghanistan Police Training and Readiness*, pp. 31–2. It is important to note that the GPPO objected to the adoption of this structure in the *tashkil*. The GPPO proposed an eight-region system, designed to ensure balanced regional and ethnic representation in the commands. It perceived the transplantation of the ANA command structure as an attempt to militarise the police, with deleterious implications for the reform process. Interview with GPPO official, Kabul, 6 November 2005.

147 'Suspects Detained in Afghanistan; Police Center Opens', American Forces Press Service, 20 December 2006.

148 Islamic Republic of Afghanistan, *Afghanistan National Development Strategy: Sector Summary Report* (Kabul: Islamic Republic of Afghanistan, 2006); ICG, *Reforming Afghanistan's Police*, p. 13.

149 As of January 2007, camps had been established in Farah, Helmand, Uruzgan, Zabul, Ghazni and Kandahar; Captain Greg Hignite, 'On Patrol: Newest ANAP Graduates Provide Security in Kandahar', *CSTC-A Defense and Security Highlights Afghanistan* (CSTC-A: Kabul, 7 January 2007).

150 ICG, *Reforming Afghanistan's Police*, p. 13.

151 Benjamin Sand, 'Afghan Government Recruiting Thousands of Auxiliary Police To Battle Insurgents', Voice of America, 10 January 2007.

152 US Department of Defense, News Briefing with Major-General Robert Durbin and Deputy Minister Abdul Hadir Khalid at the Pentagon, transcript, 9 January 2007.

153 Personal communication with Western donor official, Waterloo, Canada, 19 December 2006.

154 Interview with Ustad Mohammed Mohaqqeq, Kabul, 16 June 2006; interview with Vice-President Abdul Karim Khalili, Kabul, 18 June 2006.

155 Interview with senior UNAMA official, Kabul, 17 June 2006.

156 Personal communication with Western military official, 8 July 2007.

157 Paddy Ashdown, 'International Humanitarian Law, Justice and Reconciliation in a Changing World', The Eighth Hauser Lecture on Humanitarian Law, New York, 3 March 2004, http://www.nyuhr.org/docs/lordpaddyashdown.pdf.

158 David Tolbert with Andrew Soloman, 'United Nations Reform and Supporting the Rule of Law in Developing Countries', *Harvard Human Rights Journal*, vol. 19, Spring 2006, pp. 44–5.

159 *Ibid.*, p. 45.

160 Bonn Agreement, Article II, No. 2.

161 World Bank, *Afghanistan: Managing Public Finances for Development*, p. 50.

162 Thier, *Re-establishing the Judicial System in Afghanistan*, CDDRL Working Paper No. 19 (Stanford, CA: Stanford Institute for International Studies, September 2004), p. 2.

163 Lobjakas, 'Afghanistan: EU Aid Targets Justice System'.

164 Islamic Republic of Afghanistan, Ministry of Justice, *Justice for All: A Ten-Year Strategy for Justice Reform in Afghanistan* (Kabul: Islamic Republic of Afghanistan, Ministry of Justice, October 2005), p. 13.

165 UNAMA, *Afghanistan Justice Sector Overview*, unpublished, June 2006, p. 7; interview with USAID official, Kabul, 14 November 2005.

166 Interview with senior Italian Justice Project official, Kabul, 22 June 2006.

167 Lobjakas, 'Afghanistan: EU Aid Targets Justice System'.

168 UNAMA, *Afghanistan Justice Sector Overview*, p. 10.

169 *Ibid.*

170 *Ibid.*, p. 11.

171 Interview with senior Afghan Ministry of Justice official, Kabul, 9 May 2005.

172 Interview with Italian Justice Project official, Kabul, 15 May 2005; interview with senior Italian Justice Project official, Kabul, 22 June 2006.

173 UNAMA, *Afghanistan Justice Sector Overview*, p. 11.

174 *Ibid.*

175 *Ibid.*, p. 12.

176 Interview with senior Italian Justice Project official, Kabul, 22 June 2006. It is also envisioned that a Master's of Law degree course will be offered there.

177 Barfield, Nojumi and Thier, *The Clash of Two Goods*, pp. 19–20. During a 40-year period from 1964 to 2004, seven new constitutions or basic laws were enacted, in 1964, 1977, 1980, 1987, 1990, 1992 (a proposed mujahadeen constitution) and the most recent constitution in 2004.

178 *Ibid.*

179 UNAMA, *Afghanistan Justice Sector Overview*, p. 5.

180 It is based largely on the 1965/74 Criminal Procedure Code (CPC), the Interim CPC and the Egyptian CPC; UNAMA, *Afghanistan Justice Sector Overview*, pp. 5–6.

181 Interview with Italian Justice Project official, Kabul, 15 May 2005. For instance, in the Interim CPC, a suspect can be kept in custody without trial for a month, at which time they would have to be released. The new CPC permits detentions without trial of up to six months.

182 Thier, *Re-establishing the Judicial System in Afghanistan*, p. 12.

183 Interview with USAID official, Kabul, 14 November 2005.

184 Interview with senior Italian Justice Project official, Kabul, 22 June 2006.

185 Interview with UNAMA official, Kabul, 22 June 2006.

186 UNAMA, *Afghanistan Justice Sector Overview*, p. 1. The Justice Sector CG comprises several working groups, including Law Reform, Institutional Capacity and Physical Infrastructure, Legal Education and Professional Training, Legal Aid and Access to Justice, Land Reform, Prisons and Detention Centres and the Advisory Group on Women and Children in Justice.

187 Interview with senior Italian Justice Project official, Kabul, 22 June 2006.

188 Interview with senior Afghan Ministry of Justice official, Kabul, 9 May 2005.

189 Thier, *Re-establishing the Judicial System in Afghanistan*, p. 1.

190 Carlotta Gall, 'Afghan Parliament Rejects Chief Justice Nominee', *New York Times*, 28 May 2006.

191 Thier, 'Order in the Courts', *New York Times*, 28 August 2006.

192 Amin Tarzi, 'Afghanistan: New Supreme Court Could Mark Genuine Departure', Radio Free Europe/Radio Liberty, 11 August 2006.

193 Kim Barker, 'Afghanistan's Judge of Last Resort', *Chicago Tribune*, 28 January 2007.

194 Islamic Republic of Afghanistan, Ministry of Justice, *Justice for All*, Preface.

195 *Ibid.*, p. 3.

196 *Ibid.*, p. 14.

197 The Asia Foundation, *Afghanistan in 2006: A Survey of the People* (Kabul: The Asia Foundation, 2006), p. 59.

198 Ali Wardak, 'Building a Post-war Justice System in Afghanistan', *Crime, Law and Social Change*, vol. 41, no. 4, May 2004.

199 *Ibid.*, p. 320.

200 Barfield, Nojumi and Thier, *The Clash of Two Goods*, p. 3.

201 *Ibid.*, p. 4.

202 Islamic Republic of Afghanistan, Ministry of Justice, *Justice for All*, p. 7.

203 The studies include USAID, *Field Study of Informal and Customary Justice in Afghanistan and Recommendations on Improving Access to Justice and Relations Between Formal Courts and Informal Bodies* (Washington DC: USAID, June 2005);

International Legal Foundation (ILF), *The Customary Laws of Afghanistan* (New York: ILF, September 2004); and Barfield, Nojumi and Thier, *The Clash of Two Goods*.

204 Barfield, Nojumi and Thier, *The Clash of Two Goods*, p. 22.

205 Office of the President, *President Karzai Assigns the Attorney General To Take Decisive Actions Against Corruption*, Press Release, 28 August 2006.

206 Interview with Italian Justice Project official, Kabul, 15 May 2005.

207 Sarah Lister, *Moving Forward? Assessing Public Administration Reform in Afghanistan* (Kabul: Afghan Research and Evaluation Unit, September 2006), p. 4.

208 *Ibid.*, p. 8.

209 Islamic Republic of Afghanistan, Ministry of Justice, *Justice for All*, p. 8.

210 Interview with senior Afghan Ministry of Justice Official, Kabul, 9 May 2005.

211 UNAMA, *Afghanistan Justice Sector Overview*, p. 16.

212 A significant number of these facilities were in fact rented and were not designed to serve as detention facilities.

213 'General Director of Prisons Chosen', Pajhwok News Agency, 24 January 2007.

214 This figure does not include those held in the approximately 300 smaller district-level detention facilities across the country.

215 UNAMA, *Afghanistan Justice Sector Overview*, p. 17.

216 *Ibid.*

217 *Ibid.*; interview with Italian Justice Project official, Kabul, 15 May 2005.

218 *Ibid.*

219 Marco-Toscano Rivalta and Drury Allen, *Securing Afghanistan's Future: Accomplishments and the Strategic Pathway Forward – Considerations on Criteria and Actions for Strengthening the Justice System* (Kabul: Islamic Transitional State of Afghanistan, 2004).

220 UNAMA, *Afghanistan Justice Sector Overview*, p. 19.

221 Islamic Republic of Afghanistan, Ministry of Justice, *Justice for All*, p. 5.

222 Hamid Karzai, Statement at the Tokyo Conference on the 'Consolidation of Peace in Afghanistan – Change of Order "From Guns to Plows"', 22 February 2003.

223 Quoted in Sedra, *Challenging the Warlord Culture*, p. 3.

224 Afghanistan New Beginnings Programme (ANBP), *Afghanistan New Beginnings Programme, Brochure for the Second Tokyo Conference on Consolidation of Peace in Afghanistan* (Kabul: ANBP, 15 June 2006).

225 ICG, *Afghanistan: Getting Disarmament Back on Track*, p. 3.

226 Weapons constructed locally or in the Pakistani weapons workshops that dot the border with Afghanistan were viewed as equivalent to unserviceable and rejected. Rossi and Giustozzi quote a UNAMA official as saying that 36% of all weapons collected were constructed in workshops in Pakistan (Simonetta Rossi and Antonio Giustozzi, *Disarmament, Demobilisation and Reintegration of Ex-Combatants in Afghanistan: Constraints and Limited Capabilities*, Working Paper No. 2, Series No. 2 (London: LSE Crisis States Research Centre, 2006), p. 4.

227 Sedra, *Securing Afghanistan's Future*, pp. 3–7.

228 ICG, *Afghanistan: Getting Disarmament Back on Track*, p. 6.

229 Political Parties Law, Art. 6, No. 5.

230 ICG, *Afghanistan: Getting Disarmament Back on Track*, p. 6.

231 Christian Dennys, *Disarmament, Demobilization and Rearmament? The Effects of Disarmament in Afghanistan* (Kabul: Japan Afghan NGO Network, June 2005), p. 4; Rossi and Giustozzi, *Disarmament, Demobilisation and Reintegration of Ex-Combatants (DDR) in Afghanistan*, p. 4; interview with International Organisation for Migration (IOM) consultant, Kabul, 5 May 2005.

232 Interview with ANBP Special Adviser, Kabul, 29 April 2005.

233 Interview with senior ANBP official, Kabul, 13 June 2006.

234 *Ibid.*

235 ANBP, *Afghanistan New Beginnings Programme*, p. 2.

236 The majority of ex-combatants chose the agricultural option (41.9%), with small-business support (24.6%) and vocational training (15.5%) the next most popular options. The reintegration programme cost approximately $1,200 per ex-combatant, with $700 being directly expended on reintegration packages and the remaining $500 absorbed by overhead costs (ANBP, *Afghanistan New Beginnings Programme*, p. 5). Interview with USAID DDR Program Manager, Kabul, 24 May 2005.

237 UNDP, *Afghanistan National Human Development Report 2004* (Kabul: UNDP, 2004), p. 57.

238 It is important to note that this was a self-evaluation conducted by the ANBP rather than an external actor, making its results more vulnerable to criticism.

239 Interview with senior ANBP official, Kabul, 13 June 2006.

240 ANBP, *Afghanistan New Beginnings Programme*, p. 2.

241 Interview with senior Japanese Embassy official, Kabul, 12 May 2005.

242 ICG, *Afghanistan: Getting Disarmament Back on Track*, pp. 11–12.

243 Islamic Republic of Afghanistan, *Strategy for Disbandment of Illegal Armed Groups in Afghanistan* (Kabul: Islamic Republic of Afghanistan, January 2006), http://www.diag.gov.af, p. 1.

244 *Ibid.*, p. 11.

245 The Afghan government defines an illegal armed group as 'a group of five or more armed individuals operating outside the law, drawing its cohesion from (a) loyalty to the commander, (b) receipt of material benefits, (c) impunity enjoyed by members, [and] (d) shared ethnic or social background'. Islamic Republic of Afghanistan, *Strategy for Disbandment of Illegal Armed Groups in Afghanistan*, p. 2.

246 Interview with ANBP official, Kabul, 23 May 2005.

247 The members of the committee include the National Security Adviser, Ministry of Defence, Ministry of Interior, National Directorate of Security, Ministry of Rural Rehabilitation and Development, Ministry of Agriculture, Ministry of Labour and Social Affairs, Ministry of Finance, Ministry of Commerce and Industries, Ministry of Counter Narcotics, Japan, the United Kingdom, Canada, the United States, the Netherlands, Switzerland, Italy, the EU, UNAMA, the ANBP, the Coalition and ISAF.

248 Islamic Republic of Afghanistan, *Strategy for Disbandment of Illegal Armed Groups in Afghanistan*, pp. 4–5.

249 *Ibid.*, p. 7.

250 Japan's contribution to the $35m DIAG development fund has largely been channelled through Afghan development initiatives such as the National Area Based Development Program and the National Solidarity Program, which are engaged in the provision of DIAG community-development projects. Other donors to the DIAG process include the United Kingdom, Switzerland, the Netherlands, the UNDP and Denmark.

251 Islamic Republic of Afghanistan, *11 Province Main Phase DIAG Proposal*, Islamic Republic of Afghanistan, unpublished, 5 November 2005.

252 Islamic Republic of Afghanistan, *Guidelines for DIAG Development Activities*, unpublished, 2005.

253 During the national assembly and provincial council election stage of the DIAG process, over 124 candidates submitted 4,857 weapons and 34 candidates were disqualified for non-compliance.

254 Interview with official from the DIAG Joint Secretariat, Kabul, 24 June 2006.

255 *Ibid.*

256 *Ibid.*

257 Office of the Afghan National Security Council (ONSC), *Security Sector Paper* (Kabul: Islamic Republic of Afghanistan, 2004), p. 15.

258 Mark Sedra, 'European Approaches to Security Sector Reform: Examining Trends Through the Lens of Afghanistan', *European Security*, vol. 15, no. 3, September 2006.

ADELPHI PAPERS

The Adelphi Papers monograph series is the Institute's flagship contribution to policy-relevant, original academic research.

Eight Adelphi Papers are published each year. They are designed to provide rigorous analysis of strategic and defence topics that will prove useful to politicians and diplomats, as well as academic researchers, foreign-affairs analysts, defence commentators and journalists.

From the very first paper, Alastair Buchan's *Evolution of NATO* (1961), through Kenneth Waltz's classic *The Spread of Nuclear Weapons: More May Be Better* (1981), to influential additions to the series such as Mats Berdal's *Disarmament and Demobilisation after Civil Wars* (1996) and Lawrence Freedman's *The Transformation of Strategic Affairs* (2006), Adelphi Papers have provided detailed, nuanced analysis of key security issues, serving to inform opinion, stimulate debate and challenge conventional thinking. The series includes both thematic studies and papers on specific national and regional security problems. Since 2003, Adelphi Paper topics have included *Strategic Implications of HIV/AIDS, Protecting Critical Infrastructures Against Cyber-Attack, The Future of Africa: A New Order in Sight, Iraq's Future: The Aftermath of Regime Change, Counter-terrorism: Containment and Beyond, Japan's Re-emergence as a "Normal" Military Power, Weapons of Mass Destruction and International Order, Nuclear Terrorism After 9/11* and *North Korean Reform.*

Longer than journal articles but shorter than books, Adelphi Papers permit the IISS both to remain responsive to emerging strategic issues and to contribute significantly to debate on strategic affairs and the development of policy. While the format of Adelphi Papers has evolved over the years, through their authoritative substance and persuasive arguments recent issues have maintained the tradition of the series.